To Catch
a Thief

To Catch a Thief

Richard Taylor
with
John Miles

New Wine Press

New Wine Ministries
PO Box 17
Chichester
West Sussex
United Kingdom
PO19 2AW

Scripture quotations are taken from the following version of the Bible:

NIV – The HOLY BIBLE, NEW INTERNATIONAL VERSION.
Copyright © 1973, 1978, 1984 by International Bible Society.
Used by permission of Hodder and Stoughton Limited.

ISBN 1–903725–57–7

Certain names in this book have been changed to protect the person's
identity where necessary.

Typeset by CRB Associates, Reepham, Norfolk
Cover design by CCD, www.ccdgroup.co.uk
Printed in Malta

Dedication

This book is dedicated to my mother. I know throughout your life you did what you thought best for us and for this I will always love you. There may be times when you felt that you let us down, the same could be said of us. One thing I admire about you is your ability to keep loving despite the pain; your undying love as a mother has helped me through many difficult times in my life. Mammy thank you for everything.

Contents

What others are saying about
To Catch a Thief...

"A completely real book, describing one remarkable young man's encounter with the greatest reality there is. It will be a beacon of hope to all sorts of people. Lives can change and be lit up from within by God's free goodness, just as Richard's has been."

Dr Rowan Williams, *Archbishop of Canterbury*

"Colourful, powerful, authentic – these are the right adjectives to describe this riveting story of transformation from drug-addicted prisoner to renowned pastor. Whether he is doing his burglaries, his bird, or his Bible studies, Richard Taylor's narrative is a page-turner. This is a remarkable spiritual journey."

Jonathan Aitken

"Richard Taylor's story is remarkable one. It is a story of faith overcoming despair and of hope replacing hopelessness. Richard is not alone in his achievements. However, his experiences, so eloquently expressed in this book, should be the inspiration for many thousands of young people in this country that share the problems that existed for him."

Ray Wise, *Detective Chief Superintendent, Gwent Police*

"Richard Taylor's book *To Catch a Thief* moved me deeply. The Lord plucked this young man from the fires of hell and set him alight with the fire of the Holy Spirit. What a transformation! It brought tears to my eyes. I met Richard for the first time this year. He is a red-hot evangelist, totally yielded to Jesus and I am persuaded that eventually his ministry will reach the ends of the earth. I highly recommend this book."

Reinhard Bonnke, *Evangelist*

"If you need a dynamic change in your life we recommend you read this book."

Dinah Sansome MBE, *Victory Outreach*

"Richard's story is an impressive witness to the power of the Holy Spirit . . . at a time when many offenders are trapped in a cycle of destructive behaviour, this book will bring hope and inspiration."

The Venerable William Noblett
Chaplain General, Chaplain to the Queen

Acknowledgements

John Miles: This book would not have been written without you! Thank you for your patient encouragement for me to tell my story; for the many hours spent together unravelling my memories; and for turning our taped conversations into the final manuscript. May your faithfulness be rewarded by many lives touched and transformed by God's power.

Ken Shingleton: Thank you for giving your time to visit me in prison and sharing your faith. Your honesty and courage when visiting me spoke more to me of God's love than anything else.

David and Dinah Sansome (Victory Outreach): For giving me a home and loving me as a son. You saw in me what most could never imagine and because of that I have been blessed with a great family and future.

The Gideons: Thank you for your determination to place the Bible in every prison. Its impact on my life has affected the lives of thousands of others.

To all my friends who also found Christ and shared Him with me: Alan Andrews, Colin Lloyd, Nigel Haddock, Harty, and many more.

To my precious wife Jill and my three beautiful sons Joshua, Caleb, and Jacob. Thank you for all the time you sacrifice to allow me to minister and travel. I love you all with a passion.

Finally, to my Saviour, King and Master, Jesus Christ. Words are inadequate to describe what You mean to me. I know that without You I would not have a story and the only writing would be upon my gravestone. It is through Your amazing grace that I live to tell the story of all You have done in my life.

Chapter 1

Day of reckoning

It was a sound unlike anything I had heard before. Even though I knew it was coming, nothing prepared me for its impact. It hit my senses with a finality and a shock that is difficult to explain, unless you too have experienced it. The crash of the heavy steel door against its frame echoed around the building. It was the sound of a cell door being closed – and I was on the inside. I stared at it; solid and indifferent to my feelings or those of any other person it ever enclosed. The door locked without a key and only a spy hole interrupted its blankness. My stomach knotted with fear as I wondered how I had got myself into such a mess. I also felt ashamed that I had let my mum down so badly. She had worked so hard to raise her family alone; she didn't deserve the worry and anxiety I knew she would feel knowing that, at just fifteen, the eldest of her four sons was now in jail.

And jail it certainly was. This was no hotel-like youth custody facility; the Young Offenders Institute inside Her Majesty's Prison Swansea was a real prison. It looked, sounded and smelt like one. Its architecture and geography was just like the prisons you might see on television or in films. The sounds of voices, footsteps and cell doors, like this one being closed, echoed off unforgiving fortress-like walls. Four levels towered above each other in the Victorian economy that gave us terraced houses, designed not to waste ground space – least of all on the dregs of society who had earned their incarceration. Most of my fellow inmates were on remand and not yet convicted of any crime. Yet here we were, banged up in our cells for twenty-three hours a day, conditions far worse than for adult convicted prisoners. We were only allowed outside into the exercise yard for one hour a week on Saturday morning. You did not come out of HMP Swansea with a suntan, more like the ghost of Christmas past.

As I turned to consider my new home, it was obvious that space in HMP Swansea was at a premium. Although the cell seemed ridiculously small for two people, I was not alone. My cellmate, Jason Hedgel, was already there, perhaps recalling his own emotions the first time he saw that door close. Sadly Jason is no longer with us. He, like too many who inhabited the twilight world of drugs, later died from an overdose.

My latest arrest had been for the usual list of crimes. I had been convicted of thirty offences for drug abuse, drunkenness, theft, burglary, stealing cars and violence. This had become my way of life from the age of thirteen. I had dozens of offences behind me, the seriousness of which had risen with my age. This time I knew that I was in serious danger of being locked up. I was well known to the police and the court officials in my hometown of Llanelli in South Wales. We lived in a part of the town called the Bryn. This part of the United Kingdom had more than its fair share of hooligans like me, but I stood out as one of the worst troublemakers. The time had come for me to be stopped – at least for a while.

I was accustomed to spending a night or two in the local police station cell, often at the weekend after a day of consuming alcohol and various illegal substances. I usually descended into a sort of temporary madness. It was not easy for the police to arrest me. I was foul-mouthed, abusive and as violent as I could possibly be towards them. I would have to be physically subdued, handcuffed and dragged into the police van that we called the meat wagon. I did not "come quietly". Anyone who wonders if the police earn their pay should visit some of the South Wales town centres at closing time on a Saturday night. Next stop was a police cell, into which I was thrown, still struggling and yelling obscenities. I was so crazed by drugs that I would then try to wreck my cell. Come Monday morning I was hung-over and waiting for the ride in a meat wagon to the Magistrate's Court. The food served while in the police station was appalling. Provided by Mrs Jones, an elderly lady who lived across the road from the police station, the toast was soggy, the bread stale, and the tea almost undrinkable. The police didn't spend much money on us. Unpleasant as it was, I didn't deserve anything better.

Before leaving my cell I was handcuffed for the journey to court. I shared the meat wagon with half a dozen other lads, all arrested over the weekend on similar offences. While in the cell below the Magistrate's Court I was visited by my Legal Aid solicitor, Stephen Lloyd. Numerous appearances in court meant that I was well known to Steve. He was well known to my mates and me as the solicitor who would present our situation in court in the best light and try to get us bail. This time Steve came in with his usual greeting, "Hello Rich, good to see you," and since he always had cigarettes on him, I asked him for some. I used to joke with Steve that my criminal activities had paid for his new car or this year's

holiday. The truth is, Steve had a thankless task trying to
defend the indefensible and his end of the legal profession is
far from being well paid. I really liked Steve. "I don't think it
will go well for you today Rich, you're going to get
remanded," he warned me. He said he would let my mum
and dad know what had happened. I already suspected that
my situation was bad. My young, wild criminal career was
catching up on me and I knew I would probably go to prison
this time. Steve made the usual plea about me being from a
broken home and led astray by older criminals etc. In fact, no
one led me astray, I did it all by myself. I was the one leading
others astray!

I knew that my fate was already sealed, even before I left
the police station. There exists an unofficial system of
consultation between the Custody Sergeant at the police
station, the prosecution, the Clerk of the Court and the
Chairman of the Magistrates. In fact, it had probably been
decided before this weekend. The Custody Sergeant was a
very powerful man. He would speak to the Clerk and the
result was decided before you ever entered the court. The
police knew that they could not get someone of my age
remanded to prison unless they had a long list of offences to
add to a previous bad record. They were fed up of taking me
to court only to see the magistrate let me out again. Their
system for compiling the charge sheet was to allow you out
on police bail several times, knowing that you would re-
offend while on bail. They simply gave you enough rope to
hang yourself. When the Custody Sergeant judged that you
had built up enough offences, he might consult with an
inspector if he was unsure, then he would pass the word to the
Clerk of the Magistrate's Court that it was time to put a stop
to your activities. The Clerk's job is to be the professional

advisor to the amateur magistrates and they usually take their advice. The Clerk usually followed the wishes of the police. Thus the police were in effect replacing the judicial system. They will tell you privately that this unofficial arrangement has developed because of their frustration that the official system seems unable to cope effectively with people like me. It just lets us out onto the street again with a smirk on our faces. This is how I managed to be charged with thirty offences, all on one court appearance. I pleaded guilty to them all.

Once I had learned this system, I stopped being violent and abusive to the Custody Sergeant. It was one of the other policemen who advised me to be nicer to the sergeant, because it was he who would decide how long I spent locked up. Previously, I would try my best to annoy him by kicking my cell door and making as much noise as possible. I now began saying, "Yes boss, no problem boss."

When my turn came, I was escorted up to the dock and emerged into the centre of the courtroom as all eyes turned on me. The courtrooms at Llanelli Magistrates Court are surprisingly small. It is a modern building and the furniture of the courtrooms is a series of veneered squares and rectangles. Nothing decorates the walls or relieves the functional severity of the place. First I noticed that some of my mates were there in the small space for the public to witness proceedings. This was not unusual, it was part of our routine on a Monday morning for those who had managed to stay out of custody themselves to go to the court and look at the list to see who was up before the magistrates: "Hey look, Taylor is up today. Let's go and see what happens." I looked at them and we exchanged grins. It was important always to look tough, to act as if you didn't care what happened. Bravado was the name of the game. Inside I was scared that this would be the first time that I went to jail. I couldn't think of anything that Steve could say to alter the course of events that would now unfold.

Then, as I continued to look round the court, I was shocked to see my mother there. I wasn't expecting this. I had sent a message to her with the one phone call I was allowed from the police station, but her presence was still a surprise. As she fixed her eyes on me, I couldn't look at her and turned away. I was trying not to show the shame I inwardly felt. This sad day came on top of all the other trials she had suffered in her life and she was feeling the pain. The trouble with crime and drugs is that you become numb to the effects on other people. Your world is totally self-absorbed. Only what *I* need and what *I* want this day, matters. Hurting others, even your mum who loves you dearly and has done her best for you, doesn't come into the equation. She must have felt that her difficult life had reached a new low.

It took a little less than twenty minutes for the charges to be read, me to plead guilty and for Steve to play his part. The pre-planned verdict was that I would be remanded in custody to HMP Swansea. Another young menace to society was finally off the streets and into jail. I would be remanded in custody to wait for social and probation reports, then sentenced. I knew that, for me, prison was an inevitable step along the path towards being a career criminal or, more likely, ending prematurely with an overdose. The time in prison would not make me better, only worse. It would not be a deterrent to future crime and it certainly wouldn't stop me from getting hold of as many drugs as I could afford while in jail. The closing words from the magistrate were, "Take him away." My mum was shocked; this was unexpected. She couldn't believe what was happening. She jumped to her feet and yelled at the magistrates. "You can't do this to him, he's only fifteen." Her protests were in vain and the court officers stepped in and ushered her out of the courtroom. Such minor disturbances were all part of a day's work in the magistrates court.

Back in the cell below the courts, I waited for the meat wagon to take a group of us to HMP Swansea. My few personal possessions I held in a plastic bag, sealed by the police. This was part of a token attempt to stop drugs entering the prison. It failed and I soon discovered that drugs were as easily available in this prison as on the streets of Llanelli. As we approached the prison, I looked through the small window of the meat wagon at the outside walls. It looked a forbidding place. It's supposed to. You don't really want a prison to look like a holiday camp from the outside, or from the inside. We passed through the large outer gates made of wood. As the doors closed behind us, I realised that for the first time I was seeing the inside of a prison. We were in a sort of security area with high walls each side and another set of large, more modern gates before us. This time the gates were of steel and opening electronically. We waited while the security staff inspected the vehicle. They looked under the van, presumably to check that no bomb or drugs stash had been attached. As we passed through I thought, *"This is it, this is my life from now on."* There was an inevitability about it that was accepted by all – the police, my mates, the courts, myself and probably even my Mammy. How many more times would I pass through these gates, a passenger in the meat wagon?

Once inside the second gates, we stopped and the rear doors opened. We sat in the wagon, waiting for our name to be called. "Taylor" a voice called and I responded. The voice conveyed so much more than just my name in the one word. It wasn't kind, or friendly, I didn't expect that. It wasn't unfriendly either. It was clipped, official, slightly impatient; no nonsense. It said, *"I am in charge, sonny, and you better not forget it. When I call, you'd better move."* It told me that I was now part of a system, a routine; just another young scumbag to be processed. There was coldness and indifference in the voice; I was part of a day's work for someone. From now on, when I woke in the morning, I wouldn't wonder what I would do this day; this was their world, their routine and I would conform if I had any sense. Even the crime, the bullying, the theft and drug dealing within the prison were all part of a well-established status quo. From now on it would be *"Taylor"*. Although he was part of the system, gone would be the friendly voice of Steve greeting me with "Rich, good to see you, how you doing?" He wasn't my friend, but he coped with his day by allowing a certain warmth, familiarity and human kindness into his relationships with his clients. He was officially on my side, so he might as well act as though he was. He could go home to his family at the end of his working day, having had the absolute minimum of hostility or confrontation. He didn't approve of me, or my lifestyle; he would not invite me to his barbeque and would be horrified if I dated his daughter. It was too late now for Steve's services, I was inside. Steve moved on to his next hooligan. He would make sure that another young criminal had at least one voice speaking in his defence.

Our first stop was Reception. Any similarity to a hotel started and ended with this title. Beyond the entrance door was more processing, more routine. I was scared, but I mustn't show it. I must look tough. My expression and body language had to say *"Don't mess with me boyo, or you'll get more than you bargained for, so watch it."* The prison staff had seen it all so many times before. I doubt if any of it even registered with them. I hid my fears just below the surface. I had heard many stories of life in the Young Offenders wing – many of them exaggerated or made up. I was scared of violence, rape, bullying and the hard men who were the prison officers, known to all as "screws". But the show had to go on. I had missed a lot of my education, but I was smarter than most of these lads and many of the prison officers. Living by my wits, I would survive. Even my teachers at school, on the rare times that I attended, admitted that I had intelligence if I cared to use it. So far, none of this supposed intelligence had converted into common sense.

I handed over my plastic bag of possessions; they would be returned to me on departure. Someone was completing a form which had my name at the top. "Religion?" I had none; money, drugs and hooliganism were my religion. Given the choice of Christian, Muslim, Hindu, Jewish etc., I said "Christian", simply because I knew I wasn't any of the others. The main purpose of this question was to see if you needed a special diet required by your religion. "Taylor, your number is XY791, don't forget it." "Yes, boss," I said and began repeating it over in my mind. I was then searched. At one end of the large reception area stood a row of showers without doors or curtains. The lack of privacy only added to the stress and feeling of vulnerability. I stripped off and showered. We stood there naked as a doctor gave us a brief medical examination. We often tried to get tablets off the doctor, pleading various conditions and often asking for sleeping tablets. My drug addiction was no cause for any special attention, the prison was full of addicts and all had access to more drugs inside. Officers worked at desks in the room, oblivious of our embarrassment, having to stand there starkers in full view of the whole room.

We were then issued with our prison clothes. The normal prison uniform was blue jeans and a blue shirt. The remand prisoners had to wear brown jeans. Thus you were marked out as not yet having arrived properly into the prison fraternity. They were definitely not made to measure and none of mine fitted. They were too small, too large, too tight or baggy. No one cared except me. *"Hey, I'm in jail, what does it matter?"* But somehow it did matter, to me if no one else. Worst of all was the strange feeling of having to put on underpants that had been worn by numerous others before. I kept telling myself that they had been well washed, but it still felt odd. You may think this a strange reaction from someone who thought nothing of sleeping rough and poisoning my body regularly with drugs and booze. I may have been rather dirty at times, but at least it was my own dirt and that made all the difference. My clothes and plastic bag of personal items were put in a blue plastic box. That was the last I saw of the gear I had come in with. We sat on a bench outside the door that led to the main landing, staring straight ahead. We were not allowed to talk. We heard the footsteps of the officer approaching from inside and the sound that was to become all too familiar – a large bunch of keys jangling and a lock being opened. "Come on lads, let's go." It was now time to move on from the preliminaries of reception into the main prison landing. Passing through the door, I gazed at my new surroundings and at the levels above us. The sights and sounds that that greeted me seemed strange and a little unnerving. The smell of cheap disinfectant and body odour hung in the air. After entering, we went over to the kit area to be issued with bed linen – a green blanket, plastic cup and plastic cutlery.

"This is it, the real thing: prison," I thought to myself again. Tough as I might like to act, I was still only fifteen and this was my first sight of the inside of a prison. The memory stays vividly with me to this day. My thoughts were interrupted by an officer: "Taylor, four's, cell thirteen." I hesitated, "Where is it, boss?" We always called the officers "boss". "Upstairs to your right, an officer will be waiting for you." A voice shouted down, "Come on Taylor, move it." I ran up the steps. The officer led me to cell thirteen, he opened the heavy steel door and I stepped inside.

I had been remanded for six weeks. After this, I appeared in court again to decide if I should be sent to the Crown Court, or left to the magistrates for sentence. It was decided that magistrates would settle the matter. This led to another remand of a further four weeks for reports before I was sentenced. This was really annoying, I felt that they were just stringing out the process to keep me locked up for as long as possible. The reports were written by a social worker and a probation officer after visiting me in the prison. My third appearance in court on these charges led to a community service sentence. By now I had turned sixteen, but my youth was still taken into consideration. The Magistrates' guidelines require them to consider all alternatives to a custodial sentence.

The community service took the form of maintenance work on a local cemetery on Sundays and painting places such as youth centres. Most of the time I didn't turn up for work. The failure to attend would be duly logged and form part of the argument for a custodial sentence later on, if I continued to offend. I was also required to attend therapy sessions. Some of my mates were there too. Therapy included playing pool and darts, but also times when we sat down and talked about ourselves. We even used to pass a ball round the circle, I don't really know why. I regarded it as weird and we treated the whole thing as a joke. It was one more idea someone had come up with to try to persuade us to change our ways. I don't know if it was regarded as a success. I know that with me, it made no difference at all. I was hell-bent on a reckless lifestyle that would probably destroy me in the end and I didn't care who I hurt on the way.

Chapter 2

Monkey on my back

It may seem an extreme measure to send a boy, who still has a couple of weeks to go before his sixteenth birthday, to prison. Magistrates are reluctant to do so, especially to a place as bad as HMP Swansea. However, the police had decided it was time for me to be removed from the streets. I was about to step through a doorway into the reality of an overcrowded, understaffed, ill-equipped, Victorian jail.

Going through the door from reception, we had entered the main body of the prison at level two – there was apparently a level one – which was the basement. Level two was for special category prisoners. Even in a young offenders establishment, this provision was required for paedophiles, homosexuals and those convicted of assaulting or robbing old people. The other prisoners regarded it as their duty to persecute the special category inmates. "Nonces" we called them and often shouted abuse in their direction. Far more serious was the polluting of their food. On the journey from the kitchens to level two all kinds of stuff could be added to the food, such as urine and semen. If you behaved badly, your privileges were taken away and you might be put into solitary confinement for a few days. The main problem with solitary was that your food came from the same supply as the nonces' food, and we knew what might be in it. The times that I was in solitary, I always starved myself rather than eat the food.

The walkways down the sides of each level were entirely made of steel, all painted green. A meagre attempt had been made at some time to soften the effect by adding vinyl floor tiles to the walkways. We could have done with the interior design services of Laurence Llewelyn-Bowen; a sort of *Changing Cells* – you never know, it could make a good television series. Like all other prisons of this design, the vaulted space between the walkways had a steel mesh stretched across for safety reasons. If anyone was thrown over the side – which sometimes happened as a form of bullying – they would bounce on this improvised trampoline, with nothing hurt except their nerves. It was also a convenient way of collecting all the bed linen together for the laundry.

Each morning, the first thing you heard was an officer shouting, "Come on lads, slopping out now." We reluctantly crawled out of our bunks to pick up our pots. Welcome to a new day in HMP Swansea. On each level there was a large sink in an area we called the recess, where up to eighty young men would crowd to empty their pots each morning; the smell was atrocious. As the pots were emptied and the taps ran over them, we were usually splashed as we waited our turn with a mixture of water and urine. If we needed to excrete while banged up, there was no provision other than our pots. We were not allowed out of the cells. The main reason for this was that there were only two officers on duty most of the time. Regulations did not allow any prisoner out of any cell with this level of supervision. We were supposed to use our pots, but of course, no one wanted to. One solution was to use the large notice board we all had in our cells for pinning up pictures – usually of naked women – as a screen to give us a little privacy. We would then excrete on newspaper, fold it up neatly into a parcel and throw our "parcels" out of the window. Every morning, some unfortunate was given the job of clearing up all the parcels.

The alternative was to endure the smell in that confined space for the remaining hours until slop out time, or wait until the one hour of association when we could leave our cells. Bad enough if it was your own smell, much worse if it was your mate's! To make our cells smell a little better the inmates had developed an ingenious system with a stick of shaving soap. Using a strip torn from your blanket as string, the shaving soap was suspended over your pot, so that when you used it, or washed it out, the soap acted like a toilet flush deodorant, similar to what your mum might normally install in the toilet at home. There was a bizarre anomaly in the cells concerning the use of our picture boards. We were not allowed to have pictures of totally nude women, so we used cigarette papers to cover strategic parts. These added details brought the pictures within the standards of public decency. Yet we were supposed to squat over our pots in full view and excrete. This apparently didn't offend any standards of public decency!

Only one shower a week was allowed and clothes, including socks and underwear, were changed only weekly. This contributed to the unique smell of the place. We carried wash water to our cells in a plastic bowl. At meal times we collected our food on trays from down on twos and carried it back to our cells. An hour later, an officer would call out, "Slop out, lads." And the cell door was unlocked to allow us to place our trays outside on the floor. Someone had the job of collecting the trays. It was an unpleasant job of scraping leftover food into a bucket, stacking the trays and returning them to the twos for washing. I had the job myself for a while, during a later sentence in Swansea. I even had the job of washing the trays. They were washed in boiling water and I was given special heat-resistant gloves up to the elbows for this job. There were usually some spillages on the floor and I went round with a mop cleaning up. This job helped me with my wheeling and dealing. The cell doors had no windows, just a small peephole through which I could quickly communicate. "Hello boys, got any 'bacco, need anything?" "Taylor, do us a favour, go to five and ask them if they have any cigarette papers and we'll do them a swap." The doors always had a small gap at the bottom and we could pass things under. The doors in some prisons have a small sliding door or a wired glass panel through which you can see people, not Swansea. Once inside your cell, you were effectively isolated, really banged up.

I had a shock during association on my first day inside. There was a riot. It started as a fight in one of the recess areas. We had one black prisoner and his presence was resented. Swansea prison in the early 1990s just did not have black prisoners. Another prisoner who was from London jumped him in the recess area and within seconds a riot appeared to be igniting. Perhaps the Cockney outsider was trying to get himself a little cred with the local Taffies? Never having seen anything like it before, the response I saw from the prison officers was shocking in its speed and ferocity. They knew from experience that anything like this had to be stopped within a few minutes or it could escalate out of control. The alarm was sounding throughout the prison wing and this noise combined with the yelling of the officers and inmates combined in a frightening din.

Within two minutes, about thirty officers in full riot gear were running down the walkways towards the trouble spot. They were a blur of helmets, shields and batons. The walkways shook as they charged. Most of these officers were big strong men who would flatten a fifteen-year-old like me with a single swing of their baton. I might have been tough for my age, but I wasn't quite ready for these armour-plated heavyweights. I didn't know what to do or where to go. The rule was that if you were an innocent bystander, you indicated this by standing with your back and arms pressed flat against the wall, not impeding the charge of the hastily assembled riot squad. I didn't know this, but fortunately someone who knew it was my first day grabbed me and pulled me back against the wall, my heart pounding. I was on level two and after a few minutes an officer, wanting to make sure I was kept out of things, threw me into an open dormitory cell with four nonces inside. I didn't know whether to be more afraid of the riot squad or them; it was an uncomfortable moment. The officers soon had everything under control and they now had a good story to laugh about over their pint in the pub afterwards. It was all in a day's work.

The prison was cold. Everything about it was cold. The walls were cold to the touch, the steel walkways were cold, the air was cold. It didn't warm up much in the summer. There was no heating, not even in the coldest winter. It wasn't that the officers didn't turn the heating on, the whole block simply had no heating system. I thought this sort of thing only happened in Siberian Gulags. You just shivered, morning noon and night. You had to get an extra blanket or you couldn't sleep. I slept in my clothes.

Within my first few days in prison, I became one of the traders in drugs and cigarettes, using the skills acquired already outside. Opportunity for this trade was limited, being banged up for all but one hour a day. Slopping out time was a chance to run round and do some hurried business. I employed someone to do my slopping out for me and fill my water bottle; this gave me a few minutes. I paid him with a small amount of drugs; it was a sort of business overhead. He was my scivvy; that's what we called lads who chose this way of earning their drug supply. I also obtained supplies of drugs whenever my girlfriend visited me. Most drugs enter British prisons this way. If you lost your privileges for bad behaviour, part of the penalty was to go onto closed visits. You spoke to your visitor behind a glass screen with the aid of a telephone. This was a punishment more severe than it first appears. Your visitor couldn't pass you any drugs, your main supply route was cut off. It was really bad news.

It was visitors that usually brought drugs into the prison. We had a system which we called *plugging it*. The visitor would bring the cannabis or tablets already wrapped in a tight little cling-film parcel. This would be covertly passed to the prisoner during the course of the visit. The prisoner would then look round to see if he was being watched and if it looked safe, would unzip his trousers and quickly reach under his crotch and insert the plug into his rectum. Most of the prisoners became very skilled at this and could perform the manoeuvre with amazing speed and dexterity. The plug was retrieved later at the prisoner's convenience.

Most of the fears I had of prison soon evaporated. I quickly adapted to the routines and settled down to my new existence. I already knew a lot of the lads on the wing. I took my place among them and we shared the normal camaraderie of young men, laughing and joking. Our contact was mostly limited to slopping out, collecting meals and association, but we made the most of it. We had two aims while inside: to do our time without it getting us down and to consume as much drugs during that time as we could lay our hands on. The trading of drugs, apart from the need to satisfy the habitual craving, also occupied the minds of boys who had little else to think about. Being banged-up twenty-three hours actually fed the whole problem. Minds were thinking, planning, scheming, imagining and thus gaining some much-needed interest in life, all revolving around drugs. Where to get your next fix? This was priority business of the day.

In all my time in prison I never had a single night without drugs. I would tax the more vulnerable and sometimes even the less vulnerable prisoners. This was pure extortion based on physical bullying. If my cellmate Adrian and I knew, or suspected, that a certain prisoner had drugs available, he could be our target. "Look here you, sort us out or we will beat you up." The threat was usually enough. It may seem strange that I was able to build up my own regime of drugs supply within days of entering the prison. The reason is that I already knew half the boys in the block anyway. I already had a reputation for toughness and I was able to immediately slot into my proper place in the hierarchy of the prison microcosm.

One stroke of luck was that my mate Jim Davies was already in the prison. Jim, like most of my mates from that time, is dead now. Jim was a big lad who looked and acted tough. He was considered to be really hard and enjoyed the high position in the pecking order this afforded him. However, with Jim it was all bluff. He wasn't tough at all and I knew this, and Jim knew that I knew. I could beat him up and he was afraid of me. More than this, he was afraid I would give his little game away and go round telling everyone. *"That Jim Davies is nowhere near as hard as you all think he is, see, and tell him I said so. If he wants to argue about it, he can come and see me and I'll sort him out."* This gave me a hold over Jim that I was able to exploit. It was like when someone holds a place for you in a long queue. You can saunter up to the queue and take your place just in front of them. I slotted in above Jim Davies, saving me a lot of time and hassle proving myself. Jim was running a lot of things in the jail and I could say to him, *"Jim, do this for me or that for me"* and he would. Everyone around noted this and my cred immediately soared above big Jim. I was blackmailing him with the unspoken threat of calling his bluff in front of everyone. Jim just couldn't afford to let this happen, so he toed my line nicely.

During the long hours banged up in my cell, I had time to think. Drugs were the main mental occupation, but sometimes I lay on my bunk and wondered about my life. I was not surprised to be here, nor was anyone else. I belonged to a culture where this was just another step on the ladder of life. I thought a lot about Mammy and the pain life had dealt her. I was not a good son, far from it. I wondered if my life could have been different, but I doubted it.

If anyone was caught with drugs they would be punished by loss of privileges. Apart from the isolation cells over in the adult block with the questionable food additives in the diet, the five pounds allowance would also be stopped. So this is how I passed the days, head down, wheeling and dealing, doing my bird without too much trouble or complaint, waiting until I was let loose again into society. Sure I would prefer to be out of jail than in, but if I had to be in, I wouldn't fret about it. I would accept it as an inevitable part of the lifestyle I had chosen. The monkey on my back had to be paid.

Chapter 3

Life in the Bryn

I have few memories of my childhood compared to most people. Of the ones I do have, many are bad. My childhood was short and contained more than my fair share of grief. My Dad, Brian, was in the building trade as a hard working roofer and builder. He met my mum, Janet Thomas, locally and it wasn't too long before Mammy was pregnant with me. I was born a few months before they married. In 1975 there was a stigma to having a child "out of wedlock". The accepted thing to do was to get married as soon as possible.

The problem for my parents was where to live. They couldn't afford to buy a house and there was a long waiting list for council houses. The way to progress up the list was to gain points. Points were gained with the passage of time and through your circumstances. My parents began their married life living in a small caravan on a site by the river, near the bridge that carried the main road. After some months, they moved in to live with my Dad's parents. Mammy desperately wanted her own place and frequently made a nuisance of herself at the housing department's offices in town. When Mammy became pregnant again, it was enough for the

Llanelli housing department to give us a typical three-bedroom house on the Bryn estate, three miles from the town centre. The rooms were adequate and we had a garden. The brickwork was covered with a rendered finish, painted a colour that might have once been white. The Bryn had narrow roads barely wide enough for two vehicles to pass. They had been built in an age when ordinary working people had not been expected to own cars. When the weather was reasonable, large numbers of children played in the streets and most people seemed to know each other, at least by sight. Even then, the estate was known for crime, hooligans and drug dealing. It was a very working class area and the expectations of the people were low. Unemployment was high and this helped to generate a culture of poverty and crime in many of the households on the estate. These were the streets in which I played as a boy.

Mammy gave birth to another three boys, Andrew, Mark and Robert. With comparatively fewer vehicles around in those days, and no fear of paedophiles, we were allowed to run the streets, but not go alone into town. My brothers and I were a formidable quartet at finding, making and inventing trouble. We were a handful for our parents by any standards. The only real role models were the older boys who were already drifting into crime and drugs. These were the ones we learned from and there was an acceptance that we would follow the same path. For me it was natural that I developed a leadership role as the oldest of four brothers.

We thought Dad was great, even though he seemed to spend most of his spare time and money in the pub. He loved cars, but he didn't have much money left over to spend on them, so he tinkered a lot with them in front of the house. The various cars that appeared on our drive fascinated me. I remember a green van he once had. He fitted it out with carpets in the back for his boys. Whenever Dad said "C'mon boys, let's go for a ride," we piled into the back with real excitement. I have very few good memories of this period of my life, but these times with Dad were really good and those were times I remember most.

With Dad out of the house so much working, it was Mammy that bore the brunt of trying to control four young, boisterous lads. She tended to ignore bad behaviour as long as she could. Left unchecked, we would get worse until finally she could stand it no longer and would lash out violently at us. When Mammy lost her cool then it was time to run. Dad was the hero who never smacked us and occasionally took us out for some fun. He even tried to defend us against Mammy when she got mad.

I only remember a few holidays and these were usually with Mammy. Dad would stay at home. I remember one holiday when she took us on the ferry to Ireland. The ferry was an adventure playground unlike anything we had seen before. We rushed around causing havoc wherever our legs took us. It wasn't long before an announcement came over a public address system: "Will the parents of the Taylor boys come to the office." Members of the crew had detained us as we attempted to explore the engine room. On another holiday with Mammy we went to a budget caravan site called "The Shore". We found some red paint and brushes; this was too tempting to resist. Early the next morning we painted caravans, the insides of washing machines, washing hanging out to dry, tents, windows, even cats and dogs that were around; all were painted red. It was modern art at its best. We were all quickly expelled from the site.

My parents' marriage was in serious trouble. Mammy had

a growing resentment of the lifestyle Dad was living. The family had the money to buy the things we needed, it just went to waste in the pub. Probably my worst childhood memories are of fierce rows between my parents. Dad would come home from the pub and Mammy would be waiting for him, full of pent up anger. We would be locked in our bedrooms and would sit there crying because of the violent row going on downstairs. In many ways, Mammy treated Dad like she treated us. She would put up with a lot of unhappiness, loneliness and poverty, then, when it became too much, she would boil over. That was her temperament. When she boiled over, Dad was in big trouble. It was an emotionally destructive thing for us young children to have to witness these confrontations between two people we loved. We just didn't understand what was going on.

The break up finally came when I was nine years old. One night my mum was so furious with Dad that she threw all his clothes out of the window and locked the doors from the inside. Dad stood outside for a time shouting obscenities, but my mum was determined and just sat through the abuse. The neighbours were used to such disturbances in the Bryn; it came with the territory. Dad could have smashed his way in, but perhaps he was unsure of what might greet him if he did. He gathered up his clothes and went to stay with his mother. That was effectively the end of my parents' marriage. The divorce was completed about seven months later. Strangely, all these years later, my mum and dad have once again become good friends. If my mum is short of money, or needs a lift somewhere, Dad is always ready to help. We hoped at one time that they might get back together, but it hasn't happened. I think too much bitterness has passed between them.

Mammy had her boys and she had her house, but no husband. Some women would settle for that; two out of three maybe isn't so bad. The one problem that remained was poverty. We were now on social welfare which provided food and housing but virtually nothing else. Mammy always tried to make Christmas a special time for us even though she couldn't afford it. One year sticks in my mind as a real low point of my childhood. I must have been ten or eleven at the time. Like all children of our age, we would wake early on Christmas Day. This year we came downstairs at about five in the morning. We were dumbfounded. There were no toys. We just couldn't believe it; nothing except a few old, second-hand toys. Mammy was so broke and in debt to the loan sharks already, that she couldn't buy us anything for Christmas. We had tinned Irish stew for Christmas dinner. I don't know who was more upset by it, Mammy or her boys. It only made me more determined to steal the things I wanted.

After that year, Mammy was determined that we would have a good Christmas, with bikes and other presents, no matter what the cost. It may have been on questionable credit, but the toys were there the next Christmas. Mammy always did her best for us and going into serious debt was her way of showing she loved us. She would build up huge debts that she had no way of paying back. She desperately wanted her boys to be happy. From that aspect she was a wonderful mother. Sometimes I would watch her in the evenings. She would sit and worry about her debts and begin to cry. She was trapped in her own personal prison of debt, sorrow and disappointment. Her only happiness in life was to see us enjoying the toys that she bought for us.

I started stealing when I was twelve. At first it was mainly toys that Mammy couldn't afford to buy. My brothers and I saw nothing wrong in this. As we grew older, Mammy's control over us – which was never much – lessened and I grew wilder. My anger with the world around me multiplied. Mammy's reaction to this was strange. No matter how bad we were, she always defended us. If anyone came to complain about us, or if the police made one of their frequent visits to the house, she always defended us vigorously. "What, my boys doing that? Don't be ridiculous, they would never do anything like that. My boys are good boys." It was another way – perhaps misguided – of Mammy trying her best to show us that she loved us.

If anyone dared touch us, Mammy would go ballistic. I can recall her saying to people, "Don't you dare touch my boys, don't even think about it." On one occasion we had been throwing stones at a neighbour's greenhouse. He came to complain to my mum. We just kept insisting that we hadn't done it or anything like it. "No Mammy, we didn't, we didn't, honestly we didn't." Later I went back to the neighbour and made fun of him and taunted him because Mammy had believed us and not him. This was too much for him and he slapped me. I ran home crying to my mum. "Mammy, he slapped me, he slapped me." Mammy marched to his house and knocked the door, then punched him as hard as she could in the face when he opened it.

There was another contributing factor to my growing wildness. My mum was now a very lonely woman. The love that she longed for had always eluded her. Her failed marriage, even these boys who she tried so hard to love, seemed to do their best to hurt her. She sought consolation in other relationships. Other people came into our house and I hated it. My reaction was extreme. My behaviour deteriorated and no one could control me. I would fight, steal, hurl abuse and cause criminal damage that was shocking for a boy my age. Many people were afraid of me. The relationships that my mum had were, for me, like pouring petrol on a smouldering fire. I was angry and hurting and the world had better watch out. For me, my parents' separation and divorce could not have come at a worse time. My brothers were younger and didn't understand too much of what was happening. At the age of ten, it did maximum damage in my life.

Worst of all for my brothers and me, our dad was gone. My one bit of fun was missing. His green van no longer sat on the drive. He was allowed to come and take us out once a week on a Saturday. This was the highlight of the week for us. We would get dressed up long before he was due to arrive and sit waiting with expectation of the great time we would have with Dad. The trouble was, he sometimes just didn't turn up. We would sit there watching the clock as the time for his arrival came and went. An hour later we would still be sitting there. When he didn't come it was just too much for me. I took it out on Mammy. I thought that she was to blame and I would become totally uncontrollable. The stage was now set for my descent into a life of darkness.

At the age of eleven I moved to Brygwyn Comprehensive School in 1986. Here I made new friendships which were very important to me. With me it was perhaps stronger than most kids my age. I just didn't want to be at home. Home was a place that made me angry. We spent a lot of time together, laughing about all the trouble that we found ourselves in at school. Our teachers desperately tried to interest us in education and keep some control over us, but without the support from home their task was extremely difficult. Teachers were very frustrated with me because they recognised that I genuinely had potential and the intelligence to do well at my studies if I was to make an effort. However, I just wasn't interested.

Jason Hoskins was my best friend at the time. We used to meet outside Raymond's Florist. We would sit on a low wall and smoke. At this stage it was just cigarettes that we stole from our parents. It was our way of showing how big we were. We chatted and laughed endlessly. When it came time for us to go to secondary school, Jason was sent to a residential school for boys with behavioural problems. After that I only saw Jason when he came home for weekends. I was saddened at the loss of my daily contact with him. Again, someone with whom I could have some fun was removed from my life for most of the time. The psychological wound inside me had a bit more salt poured on it. I suppose that I should have gone to this type of special school myself, I was certainly as disruptive as anyone.

We used to smoke round the back of the school where we could see anyone coming before they could see us, and someone was always posted on lookout. We called this spot Cancer Corner. I started smoking regularly from the age of eleven. By the age of thirteen we graduated to smoking cannabis. At weekends our dad would come and pick up his four boys to take us to the swimming baths, and he would give us pocket money. I didn't want to go swimming, so I persuaded my dad to let me go separately to the local games arcade in the town called Star Games. It is the sort of place you can see in most high streets around the country. It had all the usual attractions with flashing lights and noises from the machines. What most people do not realise is how addictive these places are to vulnerable people. Star Games was destined to play a major role in my downward spiral over the next few years.

It was in Star Games that I first met people who smoked cannabis. There were people in there that would sell the stuff to anyone, even to a thirteen-year-old boy. I remember buying and smoking my first block of cannabis. I was excited by the high that it gave me and couldn't wait to involve my mates in the experience. I was the big shot among my gang, the first to get hold of and experience drugs. It was the same when we first smoked cigarettes, you wanted to be the big man, to show off in front of your mates. Cigarettes were the first step and cannabis was the second along a dark road that had youthful bravado at one end, and serious addiction to hard drugs at the other, leading to wrecked lives and often death. It was a shockingly short journey from me controlling the drugs to the drugs controlling me.

With my friend Danny James from the lower Bryn, we started stealing cars for joy riding. My dad had already taught me to drive. I would climb out of my bedroom window onto the veranda and jump down at about two in the morning. Danny's house was near and I woke him up by throwing stone chippings at his window. We would then go looking for a car. The next few hours were spent tearing around as fast as the car would go. The car was dumped before going home.

At the age of thirteen I had become uncontrollable; my mother just couldn't cope with me any more. My attitude at home was bad and I was increasingly aggressive. One day she packed my things in a bag and took me down to the Social Services office. She just put my bag on the desk. "I have had enough of him, you have him," she said, then just walked out and left me there. It was so painful for me; I felt abandoned by not only my dad, but by my mum too. She had already had one nervous breakdown and was on the verge of another. The social services placed me into the care of foster parents. I

went to live with Roger and Maureen Richards, an absolutely
wonderful couple in their early forties. They were both
schoolteachers and Roger was a very good rugby player. He
had played for Pontypool, one of the top teams in South
Wales. They had three children of their own, a boy and two
girls. Lewis, their son, was the oldest and he was a little older
than me. I loved them all and we got on very well together.
Their well ordered home and the nine months that I lived
with them became an oasis of sanity from my crazy lifestyle.

My life instantly changed once I moved there. Roger soon
had me hooked on rugby. He took me to all the matches
and generally got me interested in sport. The surprising thing
was that I soon saw that I had an aptitude for it. The
aggression that I had developed was easily diverted into
competitiveness. I excelled at long distance running because I
was really fit to begin with. This may seem strange given my
unhealthy lifestyle, but I had youth and strength on my side
and I was constantly running from the police, police cars or
dogs. I became an expert at jumping over walls and fences. I
knew the area well and I could run long distances. Thus,
entering Roger's home and eating good food combined with
a training regime, I was ready to out-run many others in my
age group. I loved the sense of achievement in completing
long distances. I won numerous trophies and medals for races
up to seven miles in length. Roger took Lewis and me
running every morning and on Saturdays we would go to
Llanelli Athletic Club where we could run on a proper track. I
trained with weights every morning to build up my strength
and also went rugby training. And I loved it.

Overnight I stopped taking drugs and committing crime. It
was amazing what a dramatic effect the change of environment had on me. Suddenly I had better things to do with my

life. I went to school every day and my work improved. The potential intelligence that my teachers insisted was there at last began to show some results. I was moved to top-level groups in various subjects. I turned from being a thicko to a swot. Roger and Maureen were teachers themselves, so they encouraged me and helped me with my work. For the first time in my life I felt I was achieving things that pleased others. I felt valued and this was very motivating. They had a completely different way of disciplining me. They would sit me down and talk through the things I had done. It was patient and skilled discipline and had an impact on me. Their experience as both teachers and parents had honed their skills. Maureen even worked in the special school where my friend Stuart Gibbons was a pupil. She worked with the likes of me every day of the week. I felt embarrassed and ashamed of the things I had done. I found myself apologising and promising not to do it again. I realised that Roger and Maureen really liked me, just for who I was. Not only had I been taken out of the Bryn, but possibly the Bryn was being taken out of me.

During my time with Roger and Maureen they went on holiday to France and I went home for a few weeks. I immediately reverted to my old lifestyle. It seems amazing to me when I look back. Environment was everything. I was back with my mates, back at Star Games and it was as though I had never been away. Then, when Roger and Maureen came home, I went back to them and once again the change of environment brought about a change of lifestyle. It was a sort of cultural schizophrenia. Once again I was doing well in school, both at my studies and sports. One permanent change that took place in me during this oasis in my life was that, for the first time, I began to believe in myself. The confidence I feel today partly stems from that time. Others began to

believe in me and that made a difference. My self-esteem
went through the roof as I achieved things that were clean
and worthwhile. I was feeling very pleased with myself.

After nine months, my time with Roger and Maureen came
to an end. It was my own decision. From this distance it may
seem a foolish thing to have done. All I can say is that I wanted
to go home. I couldn't have wished for better foster parents,
but they were not my real parents. Mammy used to visit me
regularly at Roger and Maureen's. She was pleased at all the
things I told her, proud of me for the things I was now
achieving. She never said so, but when she compared how I
was doing there with my life at home, she must have felt a
failure inside. A certain sadness in her eyes showed. Maybe she
regretted that her marriage and home had not given me the
things that I was now enthusing about. Of my three brothers,
Andrew had also been sent to the same residential special
school where my friend Jason was. Mark, the second youngest,
was also sent for fostering. Only Robert, the youngest, stayed
at home all the time.

Something deep down inside me just wanted to go home. I
used to say to her, "Mammy, I want to come home." She had
thrown me out and it needed her to agree to have me back.
She thought that my time with Roger and Maureen had
sorted me out and that if I came back I would be different.
What Mammy had always wanted might now happen. She
would have her oldest son at home, behaving himself and
doing well at school. Mammy agreed and I returned to the
Bryn. I was back with my mates, Marcus, Toastie and
Richards. I had my own bedroom which I soon kitted out
with Bob Marley posters. I didn't want to return to my
previous lifestyle. Like Mammy, I thought I had changed.
I would carry on the progress at school, keep up the sports. I

foolishly thought that I could control the drugs, enjoy the occasional smoke of cannabis, but continue to do well at school and sport. I couldn't have been more wrong. I went straight back to my mates, the drugs and the crime. My behaviour was as bad as it ever used to be.

Chapter 4

Kid's stuff

Now, drugs were my main interest. I spent every evening with my mates smoking cannabis and trying to raise enough money to pay for it. I introduced others to the habit. My close friend Jason came home at weekends from his residential special school. He was one of the boys that I enthusiastically brought into our circle. It was my role to come up with the ideas for obtaining money, usually by illegal means.

I was fourteen, I was angry at life and my teachers couldn't get near me. I was hell-bent on pursuing anything that could give me some excitement. By now Star Games was the centre of my little world. My mates were the only people I really cared about. It was an almost instantaneous step from becoming a user of drugs to being a dealer of drugs. The fact is, for the rest of my life, I have to live with the knowledge that the very ones I cared about most are the ones I took along with me into the drug scene that would eventually bring most of them down.

We started doing garden sheds, lots of them. I could pick up power tools and bikes which I could always sell. Sometimes we would steal a car to shift stuff. We had a stash in the

woods where I would hide the gear in bags until I was ready
to sell it. This was behind the local Elim Pentecostal church.
Sometimes I would sell stuff at the pub my dad used, The
Smith's Arms. I knew most of the men there. Dad knew that I
was stealing gear and used to tell me off for it. Once I found a
wallet with about forty quid in it. Dad took the wallet off me.
That didn't stop him from spending the money in the pub.
Parked vehicles were frequently a target. We often found
cigarettes, cash and stereos, anything that would provide us
with money.

Most nights I met my mates in a local subway that ran
under the main Cardiff to Llanelli road. We smoked the
cannabis that I had purchased in Star Games earlier in
the evening and had a laugh. We were all from the same
school and it was our disruptive antics in school that were
often the source of our amusement. If I wasn't at the subway,
I would be on the steps outside Star Games. These three steps
became my regular spot for dealing drugs. I called it my
"office". At weekends it was always Star Games.

I spent more and more time at Star Games, out of school
hours and frequently when I should have been in school. There
I began mixing with older people in their twenties who were
more experienced in the drug culture. My childhood was
coming to a premature end and I couldn't wait to grow up. My
new friends had access to drugs other than cannabis. From
them I obtained speed, an amphetamine in powder form that
can be swallowed or snorted – my preferred way of taking it. I
snorted it through a rolled up ten pound note. It was sold in
small quantities at ten pounds a time, enough for one wrap.
The effect of this drug is both physical and mental. You get a
physical rush and feel very alert, confident and alive. The
trouble was, like all drugs, it didn't last. When you come down

from the effect of the drug, it does not leave you normal, but feeling down and craving for your next bag.

I had no fear of the police or the courts because I was under the age of fifteen. The police couldn't do anything to me and I knew it. This was petty theft and hooliganism and they don't lock up children – as I legally was – for that type of offence. We were just given a verbal slap on the wrist and told not to do it again. They would usually impose a Social Services Supervision Order and a social worker would start visiting your family. Between the ages of thirteen and fifteen I was arrested and appeared in juvenile court more times than I can remember. The charges were usually theft, burglary, criminal damage or taking away vehicles without the owner's consent. All of my mates were the same, all knew that we could get away with almost anything. Sometimes we would take the rap for older mates, confessing to crimes of which they were guilty, in exchange for money or drugs. They wouldn't have to go to jail and we wouldn't either. It was a win-win situation for everyone. Except, of course, the victims of the crime.

As I approached the age of fifteen, I started drifting away from my own age group and hanging around with older mates in Star Games. I began experimenting with other drugs. An easy to obtain and effective combination was to take various sleeping pills with alcohol. One effect of this was that it enabled you to stay awake and consume more alcohol. We had various phrases that we used for the effects of drugs, such as "off your face", "stoned" or "smashed in your head". I graduated to a gang of older men who called themselves "The Town Boys", who were dedicated to terrorising the town. We were really evil. We enticed lots of youngsters into drugs, destroying their lives. We were violent and ruthless.

We all had a tattoo of a cannabis leaf on our forearm – it was a sort of membership badge.

My daily intake of drugs cost a lot. I needed to raise at least a hundred and fifty pounds a week to buy them. Money had to be obtained by whatever means. Stealing became a way of life. I began by stealing from my mother, who had very little to start with. I often stole to order. Bikes were popular. *"You want a bike? What sort? How much can you pay? No worries, I'll get you one very cheap."* My career in crime had begun young. The older guys would teach me how to raise money. One of the first trips I did with the town boys was to Tenby. Because it was a popular seaside resort, it had several games arcades with lots of slot machines. We spent the Saturday robbing the slot machines, which we had learned how to break into in a matter of seconds. We could then lift the front a little and reach inside to operate the small levers that allowed the pound and fifty pence coins to drop down, chung chung chung, into the front tray as winnings. The machines are far more secure these days. Sunday was spent smoking cannabis.

Caravan parks were another favourite, especially out of season. The owners kept a lot of things in the vans during the winter. We stole televisions, radios and anything else worth selling. We would sell stuff to anyone who wanted the goods, but our most frequent customers were the drug dealers themselves. They were in business and had lots of contacts to sell goods on to. Usually we would just exchange the gear directly for drugs. We soon learned what the dealers were willing to take. One big dealer would always take video machines. This dealer never worked, but had new cars, a speedboat, a big motorbike and a house full of class stuff. When he was finally busted by the police, they took the lot. He lasted as long as he did because he was very careful.

You parked opposite and knocked at the door. He would be watching who approached. If he didn't know you, he wouldn't sell to you. He would deny that he had anything, in case you were with the police. "What are you talking about? I don't do that stuff." I stood at his door demanding stuff until he sold me what I wanted: "I know you do this stuff, now come on, sort me out."

Burglary was a quick and easy way to steal. By this time I needed a much higher income to support my habit. My first burglary was with an older mate we called Cheeks. Like so many others, sadly he is dead now. Almost all the burglaries were during the daytime after school, while the house-holders were at work. Cheeks checked that the house was unoccupied by ringing the front door bell. When there was no answer, we went round the back and climbed over the gate. Cheeks had a small bag in which he carried his burglary kit. Part of this was a roll of masking tape that he quickly applied to a pane of glass in the door, to be able to smash it silently. It was then simple to reach through and release the lock and bolt. It took less than a minute to gain entry into the house. He then told me to "spin" the ground floor while he spinned the upper level. This was the term we used for a rapid search of the property. I was really scared. My heart pounded and I was sweating. It was unfamiliar territory, I didn't know whose house it was, I worried about someone coming home, but I pushed these thoughts to the back of my mind and raced round the ground floor looking for cash and jewellery. These items were the main target for anyone trying to fund their daily drugs purchase. This house seemed to belong to an elderly person. Older people tend to keep their cash at home and not in bank accounts. Cheeks soon found cash and some jewellery. I found quite a large quantity of sleeping tablets that the householder had been getting on prescription from the doctor but not using. This was a real bonus because the burglary had immediately yielded drugs. We then left by the same door. It was all over in a few minutes. Cheeks gave me some of the cash and we split the jewellery.

Subsequently I did a few more burglaries with older men who showed me the various techniques used in their crimes. One of them was my first commercial property, which was a shop in the town that sold very expensive items. Before my crime career was over, I would break into many of the commercial properties in Llanelli. However, I soon realised that I needed to work on my own and take all the money to support my drugs habit. Petty cash was high on my list when deciding which shops to burgle. Hairdressers were a favourite because they usually had between fifty and a hundred pounds in their petty cash. With a bit of experience, I could usually find it fairly quickly. Any machine that took cash, such as a pay phone, was an immediate target. I would tear it off the wall and smash it open. Once I opened a payphone to discover that it was stuffed with banknotes. The owner of the premises was using the phone's cash box as a secure place to leave money overnight. I was rather pleased with that little bonanza.

Gradually the burglaries became more audacious. After leaving town one night pretty drunk, I had no money for my next day's drug intake and needed to get some cash quickly. Walking towards home with my mate Adrian, we spotted a funeral parlour. Don't ask me what I was thinking, but something kept saying, "Maybe there's money in there?" The door was solid, but we kept ramming it with our bodies until it started to splinter. After ten minutes we were in. The place was dark, which freaked me out a bit, after all it was a funeral parlour. I turned to Adrian and told him to start checking the coffins! There were no bodies there, just ready-made coffins, but he argued with me, "Taylor, there's no way I'm touching one of those, man!" So we scanned the place for potential gear and came across several long black Crombie coats that we could easily sell to the right buyer. Hauling them out of a cupboard we discovered piles of black shoes, mainly brogues, so we bagged them up and carried them out.

The next day there was a knock on my door. It was the police. In our drunken state of the night before, we had been dropping shoes out of one of the bags which had split. We had more or less left a trail of shoes that led to my door for the police to follow! However, we had managed to stash the remainder of the gear in a nearby garage so the police found nothing. Later we sold the coats and what was left of the shoes and got the money we needed for drugs.

Shoplifting was another important source of income. I soon learned the things that could easily be converted into cash. Video tapes, cosmetics, small electrical items such as a hair dryer. Once I had been caught a few times, I became known to the shops in Llanelli and I had to spread my activities further afield. Saturday was the big day for shoplifting. I would take the train to Camarthen or Swansea, where I had a stash. This was mainly bags that I needed to carry the items I had stolen. Joints of meat were popular items. I would go to a super-market and clear a whole shelf of meat into my sports bag and quickly walk out with it. Many of the joints were on sale for seven to nine pounds each. Other customers would see me and wonder what I was doing, but before they could work things out or react, I was off. I would sell them for half price.

I sold the gear in particular pubs, known to be unofficial shops. At one pub in particular, I would go in the back door and into the bar. The landlord of the pub would lock the front door and I put out all the items for sale on the bar and conducted an auction. "I have a lamb joint here, who will give me two pounds for it? Here you are, a lovely gammon joint, who will give me one pound fifty for it? Come on Bill, finally do something useful for your wife, she'll love it. Hey George, your wife's always wanted a bit of beef from you, how about this for three quid?" They could see from the price label the bargain they were getting. The best customers were older men who would buy a joint of meat and take it home for Sunday lunch.

I sold different things in different pubs, the most notorious of which was the Denever. Closed now, this was a place full of drug addicts. Just about every crook and low life in the area drank at the Denever. It was a sort of wheeling and dealing criminal's supermarket. There were frequent police raids, but they had little effect. It was one of my favourite hangouts and sometimes I would spend the entire day there from opening time to closing time. On a Saturday, some of the younger kids would come to see me in the Denever and I would give them a list of items which, if they stole, I would buy off them. It was an arrangement that worked well. They went out and stole the gear for me, I paid them for the stuff, and then I sold it on to the punters in the Denever for three times as much, which usually covered my bar tab! Often the pub would stay open after hours, but with a closed sign on the door and heavy curtains drawn, until three in the morning. I have woken up in the morning lying on the pool table. Lots of people would sleep there. The speed increases tolerance to alcohol and enabled us to drink and drink until the speed wore off and we passed out. All this while I was still fourteen or fifteen years old.

There were frequent fights in the pub or the alley outside, especially when a gang from another town would come into Llanelli. I had crazy, mad fights with pool cues and pool balls being thrown around. A frequent cause of fights was when a dealer owed his supplier money for drugs. The small-time street dealers were often just financing their own habit and, like other addicts, lived only for the day. Rarely did they have any spare cash to buy their supplies, they bought them on credit. The dealer couldn't sell many drugs unless he allowed this arrangement. Instead of keeping the sales money to pay the debt, he would spend it or use too many of the drugs himself, not worrying about the consequences. I got into trouble myself this way. I was dealing one day on the steps of Star Games, when a car pulled up and the passenger called me over. I bent down to look in the window and was met by a fist hitting me square in the face. Another man jumped out with a cosh in his hand and attacked me. The first man picked up a gas cylinder and threw it in my face, knocking me to the ground. I still have the scar from this. Even in an unequal fight of this nature, it was important to put up a good fight and show defiance, yelling and cursing, doing your best to fight back. I yelled at them, "Come on then!" As young as I was, I was a hardened street fighter and after putting up as good a show as I could with these two, I retreated into Star Games, my own territory. I knew the escape route out through the back door to another part of town.

My level of crime, violence and drug abuse was shocking for someone not yet halfway through my teens. I was descending into a pit from which few emerge alive or sane. Cheeks was my most frequent supplier, but there were several others too. There is usually a Mr Big in the drug supply chain, but in our town it was a Miss Big – a middle-aged woman who was the drugs baroness in Llanelli. She supplied the local pushers. Rumour was the drugs came in on small boats along the coast and from there went to an estate in Swansea called Blaen-y-Maes. This notorious estate was the drugs capital of South Wales. From the same place you could buy guns and stolen cars. I didn't *want* to commit crimes, it was a necessary means to an end. I just had to have the money to buy drugs. It was the only thing in life that mattered.

Chapter 5

Me and my mates

My drug intake increased significantly after my time in care and I would come home at two in the morning banging on the door and yelling to my Mammy to let me in the house. Once again it was Mammy who bore the brunt of my behaviour. It was obvious that she couldn't cope. Even though I was bad, I loved her and eventually saw that I needed to move out.

I went to the social services and they helped me to find a bed-sit. My new accommodation in the bed-sitter didn't last long. The place was soon trashed and I was kicked out. During the next year I had three different bed-sits, none of them lasting long before I had to leave. I lived rough, often sleeping on the streets, sometimes within a few hundred yards of Mammy's house. Outside one of the local pubs was a favourite place. There was a spot in the car park, at the side of the pub, where warm air blew out from the heating system all night. It made for a better night's sleep. Sometimes I would stay with mates for a night, at a girlfriend's house, or sometimes I would persuade my dad to let me stay a night. He would make me promise to stay no longer than that, afraid of having to cope with my behaviour:

"Dad, I have nowhere to stay, can I stay here?"

"No, you will only start coming home drunk in the middle of the night."

"Please Dad, just one night."

"All right, but just one night, mind you."

"Thanks, Dad."

On rare occasions, I would even stay a night at Mammy's house. The police accurately described me as having "no fixed abode".

With the Town Boys I hung out at Star Games or a place called "The Sunken Gardens", which, ironically, is a public garden area outside the courthouse. Among this gang were Cheeks, Scott, Stu Lloyd, Roy Jenkins, Jason Gibbs, Richards, Steve James, my good friend Michael "Bunch" Morgan and many more. During the summer we occupied this area to the exclusion of honest citizens. We traded goods and drugs there with little to hinder us. We took drugs and even injected amphetamines there in the open, with normal citizens hurrying by, keeping their distance. We were so intimidating that many people were afraid to walk past us.

Sometimes we were so drunk that arguments would break out among us, resulting in fierce fights. Occasionally one gang member would badly hurt another while drunk, but then be the best of pals again the next day. Bunch had his jaw broken by Roy Jenkins who hit him hard with a can of beer, endways on. Bunch was back from hospital a few days later with his jaw wired up and they had a good laugh about it – although Bunch's capacity for laughing was at this time rather restricted. I overdosed a few times in the Sunken Gardens and passed out. The boys would go to one of the shops and borrow an empty dustbin, fill it with water from the fountain and pour it over me to wake me up. This usually worked and they knew that I had got away with it. If I hadn't woken, then they would have known it was serious and called an ambulance.

On one occasion, Scott and I were sitting on a bench in the Sunken Gardens thinking up ways of making money to buy drugs. Another mate, Big Jim Davies, came by on his way back from court. We needed several grand to tide us over for a few weeks; I kept thinking, "Where can we get that kind of money from?" until the answer came to me: the nearby Post Office. I worked hard to convince Jim that turning over the Post Office was a fantastic opportunity to make plenty of money quickly. There was no way I was going to risk carrying out an armed robbery myself, but lining someone else up to do was OK. I convinced Jim to go along with the plan.

In the absence of a firearm being available, Scott provided us with a baseball bat for the job and I provided a balaclava. We gave Jim instructions about what he was to do and then Scott and I positioned ourselves about three hundred yards away from the Post Office and sent him in. His brief was to storm in and threaten violence if they didn't hand over the money. Jim went in and several heart-pounding seconds later alarm bells began ringing. As fast as we could, Scott and I legged it back to the park and tried to look as innocent as possible.

From the park we could hear the sound of police sirens and screeching tyres. Wondering whether Jim had managed to make his escape we were horrified when seconds later he appeared out of nowhere and came running towards us! "Jim," I cried, "get the hell away from us, man!" We didn't want to be seen with him for obvious reasons so we threatened to beat him up if he didn't leave us immediately.

Later we discovered that the postmaster had refused to give Jim any money and sounded the alarm. Jim had begun smashing the place up until finally making a run for it when he realised he wasn't getting anywhere. He left with nothing but was later arrested and successfully convicted for the crime. He got seven years.

Although I burgled numerous shops, the real money was in houses. Electrical goods, jewellery, cash, chequebooks or bank Giros. Because of the poor economic state of Llanelli at this time, a lot of people were on social security benefit and received their money as a Giro cheque through the post each week. The recipients usually lived in cheap flats or bed-sit accommodation. In Llanelli, Giros were delivered through the post on Thursdays. I would follow up on the postman's visit to an address. The postman delivered the Giro through the letterbox early in the morning while the occupant was still asleep. I would then come along and kick the door open, just pick up the Giro and be off before the occupant had time to jump out of bed. It was a sort of residential mugging. I would then get someone to sign and cash it for me at the Post Office.

Giros and muggings often went together. They were just so easy to cash. Fortunately, the Social Security tightened up their procedures and you can't do this any more. We would mug people on the street just for their Giros or stand near the Post Office and wait for other youngsters going in, grab them and threaten serious violence unless they gave us half their money on the way out. The intimidation almost always worked and we extorted their money. We would even mug other drug addicts and steal their drugs off them. They could hardly go to the police station and complain, *"He's nicked my cannabis off me, officer."* In all this, I had no thought or compassion for the victims of my crimes. I was stealing from the poorest and most vulnerable members of the community, but I was the only person at the centre of the dark world I inhabited.

Stealing cars purely for transport rather than joy riding was one of the things I did a number of times. One night I needed to go to Kidwelly, just outside Llanelli, to get a quantity of drugs. I asked my younger brother Mark if he wanted to come along for the ride. He was only twelve at the time. I stole a Vauxhall Cavalier.

Jason Gibbs went with us because he also wanted a supply and Mark rode in the back. Suddenly, I noticed that we were being followed by a police van. It was a small van used by the police dog handlers. We were not speeding, but he must have thought we were worth checking out because he put his blue flashing light on, intending to pull us over. As soon as I saw the lights I thought, *"There is no way that you are going to catch me,"* and I floored the accelerator. It was an old Cavalier and by the time we were doing eighty the whole car was shaking. Now the adrenalin was flowing and the policeman following would also be getting a rush. He would already be on the radio calling for backup.

I knew this old Cavalier couldn't outrun the police van. I could only get away by driving more recklessly than the officer. There was a very sharp, almost hairpin bend coming up. I knew it was there. I thought that if I didn't slow down, I could gain on the van. Mark in the back was terrified, screaming at me and hanging on for dear life. Jason was also yelling, "What are you doing, Taylor?" I was yelling back, "Shut up, shut up." As I took the bend far too fast, the back end started to drift out and a crash was on the cards. I instinctively turned into the skid to straighten things up but

I was running out of road. We drifted towards the outside edge of the road and the front of the car hit a low bank. The front rose and the whole car left the ground. It flipped in mid air. For a second, it was as if the whole thing was in slow motion. We hit the road with a sickening crunch. Our forward momentum ensured that the car rolled over twice before coming to a grinding stop. The car came to rest on its roof in the middle of the road.

The policeman stopped a hundred yards back from us and immediately called for more back up and an ambulance. He approached our vehicle cautiously; after all he didn't know who was in it, how many we were or if we were armed. This gave me a few seconds to decide what to do. As the Cavalier screeched to a stop, I reached into the back through the reduced space left by the crushed roof and pulled Mark through to the front with me. I kicked with all my might at the car door until it sprung open.

We jumped out, ran to the right side of the road, pushed through a hedge of large bushes and began to run across the field. Jason couldn't run; he was trapped in the Cavalier by the damage. Later he told the police that he was just hitching a ride and didn't know who the driver was. His story couldn't be disproved. Running as fast as we could across the field quickly became a nightmare – it was a marsh. The night was pitch black. It was impossible to see where we were going. It was like one of those dreams where you try to run but your feet get stuck. Our feet were sinking with every step and we were falling into the mud then struggling back to our feet. I could just see Mark running beside me if he kept close. Concentrating on staying upright, I suddenly realised Mark wasn't with me any more, so I stopped. Breathing heavily, I called out, "Mark, where are you?" "Over here," he replied, near to tears. I located him by the sound of his voice. He had dropped down into a particularly wet section of the marsh and was in mud above his waist. I pulled him out and he was plastered. To make things worse he stank something awful.

By now more police cars had arrived and a powerful searchlight was scanning the area, trying to spot us. We just lay down flat on our faces in the long grass, effectively camouflaged by the mud that now covered us. We thought we might wait it out there until the police gave up and left. Then I heard the dogs barking. I began to panic. We had to get out of the place or the dogs would surely find us. Surrender wasn't an option that crossed my mind. Then I had an idea. We began to move to our left and forward of the police vehicles and curved back towards the road. We reached the bushes just ahead of the police cars. The scene was amazing. Lots of police cars, sirens wailing, lights flashing, dogs barking, the road blocked off and searchlights scanning the field. You would have thought that we were the great train robbers. I could hear my heart pounding. We were close enough to the police to hear what they were saying and the dogs panting. A small army of police now were taking pictures, making notes, measuring this and that, and we couldn't help but laugh. Looking back towards the police cars, we ran across the road and through the bushes on the other side. We were clearly visible in the headlights of the police cars as we dashed across, but of course they were all looking in the wrong direction. The brief seconds in the police headlights showed just how much the mud covered us. We looked liked zombies from some horror movie.

Beyond the bushes was the railway line that ran back to town. Unseen, we quietly walked on the line, past the police towards town until it reached a point where we could emerge back onto the road. We were opposite a pub, about two miles from the scene of the crash. We were laughing all the way. Our escape was just so audacious; all those police with their lights and dogs and we had outwitted them. We went into the pub to phone a taxi. As we entered, the whole place stopped and went quiet as every eye turned on us. We must have looked a bizarre sight to the regulars having their pint. We were not only covered with mud and green slime, we stank to high heaven. I said, to no one in particular, that we just wanted to use the phone. Perhaps the customers were so relieved we hadn't come to stay for a drink, that no one asked us any questions. The taxi came and took us close to our house. We jumped out and did a runner – we never paid for taxis. Once home we showered, changed and threw the dirty clothes away. We laughed about the adventure for days.

Chapter 6

Out again

At the end of my remand period I was returned to court for sentencing. I received a community service order imposed by magistrates. I had tasted real prison for the first time. I had just turned sixteen and the magistrates were reluctant to impose a regular custodial sentence. After sentencing, I had to return to the cells. Steve, my solicitor, came down to see me. He sat down and gave me a couple of cigarettes. We congratulated each other. It was a victory for us, community service rather than going back to the prison for a custodial sentence. We were both overjoyed; my joy was real, Steve was doing his thing. I was buzzing, "Yes, yes!" I kept saying. After some formalities, I was released. My mates were waiting for me. "Hey, there's Taylor. How you doing Taylor?" They had checked the list for that day and saw my name was up. "Great to see you guys, I've just got to go in here and sort a few things out, I'll see you later down Star Games." "Yeah, see you later, Taylor."

For young criminals still in our mid-teens, having done bird was a great status symbol. Now I was a minor celebrity for a while. Many of my mates hadn't been inside and I had. This gave me respect among the people I cared about, pushed me much higher up the pecking order. As I bounced into Star Games, the lads would say to each other in a lowered tone, "That's Taylor, he's been inside." Because I was classed as having no fixed abode my release grant was a Giro for £200. I immediately blew this on drugs, new trainers and new trousers. I had to look the business for my big celebration. When I saw my mates, it was one big party. I paid for nothing, my mates treated me to free booze and drugs. I was definitely the man. By the end of the evening we were completely off our faces with both booze and drugs. *"Welcome home Taylor."*

With the fear of prison largely gone from my mind, it was with renewed determination that I pursued my career of crime and to hell with the consequences. One crime that stands out in my memory was with my brother Mark. For several weeks I had been clocking a chap walking down Station Road to his ground floor maisonette in an area called Old Lodge. It was a bit strange, because I had noticed him carrying small bags of cash to his maisonette. They looked like bags containing a considerable amount of coins. It was a Friday afternoon and I had followed him a couple of times. I noted where he worked and even followed him through the security door of the block of maisonettes. Getting as close as I could without arousing his suspicions, I spotted the door that I was fairly sure belonged to his place. I had no idea why he was hoarding coins in his maisonette or how much was stored inside. It was too good an opportunity to miss, but I needed some help.

I decided to bring my brother Mark in on the job. I said to him, "Mark, I've got a bit of an earner here for us. It's a simple job and I know there is money in the house. We're in, we're out, cash, and we're gone, okay? I don't know how much we're going to make, but a good whack." I told him the plan. One afternoon we cautiously approached the maison-ettes. I quickly opened the outer security door with a screwdriver and we went to the door that I was pretty sure was our man's. It was a solid door but had a pane of glass to the side of it. I kicked this in and Mark squeezed through and opened the door from the inside. Once inside I said, "Mark, you spin the front room and I'll do the bedroom." I quickly found what we had come for – the bags of cash were in the wardrobe. Now I was buzzing. I looked into some of the bags and was surprised to see banknotes too. This was a real find.

We grabbed the bags and walked out with them. They were really heavy. I took the heaviest of the bags. Outside the sun was high and it was hot. Within a short distance we were tired and sweating profusely. The nearest place we could stash the bags was about three quarters of a mile away at Mammy's house. We had no alternative but to grit our teeth and take the pain. We must have looked an odd sight, struggling along with what anyone could see was bags of cash, in mid-afternoon. People stared at us as we passed, but no one said a word. We counted it and the total was seven hundred pounds – a lot of money to us. In Mark's room, I pushed his rug aside and lifted a loose floorboard. We stashed the bags in there, replaced the board and the rug, feeling very pleased with ourselves. After this, whenever we wanted money, we went and dipped into our little hoard.

I now felt very rich with this large amount of cash at my disposal. I purchased a large block of cannabis and treated my friends down at the Circles pub to a couple of joints each. For a while I was the generous pal with plenty to give away instead of scheming how I might get hold of my next fix. This windfall made me all the more determined to pursue crime. After all, I was obviously so successful at it.

My best mate from the age of sixteen was Bunch. We did everything together. Occasionally we would fight when we were drunk, but we were really good friends. His dad had died at an early age. He was about four years older than I was, but it didn't make any difference to our friendship. At 9 o'clock sharp every morning Bunch would knock on my door. Our first call was always to Victoria Wine when we would buy two flagons of cider. If it was prescription day, we would go first to the doctors, followed by the pharmacist. I was always on something, usually Valium. Whatever the day, we went next to the indoor market in the centre of Llanelli. We would sit on a bench, take some tablets and drink the cider. This was our breakfast routine to get the day started. The drugs and alcohol counteracted the hangover effect of whatever we had taken the night before and cleared our heads enough for us to begin to think about the day ahead. Addicts only live one day at a time.

We then began to plan the day: how we would get some gear, where would we steal the money and who we would go to see. In the absence of plans more sophisticated, we would resort to crude forms of robbery. We had to come up with some ideas. We never even considered the option of not getting the money. If we hadn't a better idea, we would take higher risks and just stop people in the streets and extort money from them. Sheer aggression was one of our most frequent methods. Other teenagers were the easiest targets, especially in Star Games where we had the added confidence of being on our own turf. *"Hey you, give us a tenner or we'll slap you all over the place."* It almost always worked. Saturday was the best day. Star Games had all kinds of games and amusements that attracted youngsters. We would just quietly move from one target to another, gathering money until we had what we needed. Later in the day, as the shops had more customers, we would go shoplifting. I usually dressed in my waxed fishing jacket that had large pockets, and a woollen hat. Boots was a favourite place for things like blank video tapes. These could always be easily sold.

I remember a shop burglary we did together one night. The weekend was almost upon us and we had no cash to buy our weekend supplies. As usual, Bunch relied on me to come up with most of the ideas. I said to Bunch, "I've been thinking about that car accessories shop in Station Road, Bob Fowden's, I bet that's loaded with gear that we can flog easily." "Can we get in?" Bunch asked. "We'll try round the back. We can probably get in through the flat above it."

It was in a row of shops that occupied the ground floor of old Georgian buildings with very steep slate roofs. On top of the shops there was a flat, but above the flat was a steep roof that had the "V" of the gable end facing onto the road. The roof contained an attic room with a small window also facing the road. The shape of the roof was significant to later events.

We went round the back and discovered the fire escape that led to the first floor flat. It didn't look as though it was occupied.

"This is it Bunch, let's do it," I urged.

"I dunno Taylor, it looks a bit dodgy to me."

"C'mon man, it's cool, let's go."

At the top of the stairs there was a small window. I smashed it with my elbow and removed the rest of the glass. It was big enough for us to squeeze through. We were in a room used for storage and we soon found the stairs leading down to the shop. "I told you it was cool man, we're in. Easy, see?" I wondered why a shop that specialised in selling electrical gadgets, even alarm systems, didn't have the premises better protected. Suspicious, I warned Bunch to go carefully in case there were movement sensors. He moved ahead of me. "Let's go down man, it's all right." Reaching the bottom step he trod on an unseen triggering device in the form of a pressure pad. Without warning, the whole shop lit up like Blackpool illuminations. Worse than this, an alarm sounded with a frequency and volume specifically designed to disorientate the human brain. There was no ignoring it while we grabbed a few things, we just put our hands over our ears and ran back up the stairs chased by two hundred pulsating decibels. Once back outside on the landing we tried to clear our heads and calm shattered nerves. Just as we were regaining our senses we heard other sirens, this time from approaching police cars. They must have been patrolling the area and heard the noise. The whole town centre must have heard the noise!

I thought our best escape route was over the roofs of neighbouring properties to find another way down. Bunch wasn't quite so athletic as I was, but with some hesitation he followed. Progress down the row of shops would have been hopelessly slow if we climbed up and down every one of the steep gable roofs, each one the height of a room. I scrambled up the first, sliding back half a step for every one I climbed. Swinging my legs over the apex, I saw how high it was, more than three storeys. Adding to the urgency, one of us had been spotted by the police below. I realised we could speed our progress considerably if we leaped across from this roof to the next without the climb down to the valley and back up.

"Bunch, let's jump it," I yelled.

"Taylor, what are you talking about, man?"

"We'll jump it."

"Oh Taylor man, I don't know if I can do it."

"C'mon man, if I can do it, you can. Watch me and you follow, okay?"

With that, I leapt across to the next roof. I was careful to land flat against it, spreading the weight to both arms and legs. This way I avoided breaking the ancient slate roof. I reached up and grabbed the apex and hauled myself up. I turned and looked at Bunch. His face gave his thoughts away – he looked very doubtful. The police were closing in. "Come on man, quickly!" The sound of police activity below must have spurred him on. As he prepared to jump I said, "Spread your weight." But Bunch couldn't have heard me. He launched into an almighty leap and landed on the opposite roof, feet first.

He must have landed midway between two roof timbers, because he torpedoed through the slates as if they weren't there. He just disappeared. He crashed onto the attic floor below. The last I heard was his swearing and cursing as I did another impression of Batman and landed flat on the next roof. I escaped, but Bunch was arrested before being taken to hospital for stitches in his badly cut legs. He didn't grass on me.

It was around this time that I first injected heroin. I had just turned seventeen. I knew a girl who was two-timing her boy-friend and seeing me. This lad had obtained a large quantity of Palfium tablets. I think these were for controlling pain in cancer patients and were morphine/heroin based. I could never find out where he got them from, but such a quantity could only have come from a pharmaceutical manufacturer or wholesaler. Normally you couldn't get these tablets, but he had the drug addict's equivalent of a pot of pure gold. I bought them for as little as fifty pence each. I could then sell them on for up to two pounds each. I didn't make as much money as I could have because I was more interested in using them myself. I often took them in the public toilets in Llanelli town centre, just opposite the Police Station. I always carried – tucked into the top of one of my socks – my "works" or "gun". These are the terms we used for the needle and syringe for injecting. I would keep a spoon hidden behind the cistern in the toilet. It became a routine of crushing the tablet into power, mixing it in the spoon with a little water and heating it up with my lighter under the spoon. When the drug dissolved, I pulled it into the syringe and injected it. This is how my friend Richard Llewelyn died. We were in the Circles pub. He had injected one tablet the day before and he didn't know the extent to which the drug was still in his body. This was a pharmaceutical preparation mixed with other things and was probably designed to have a longer effect than he was used to. He took only half a tablet the next day and it killed him – just another junkie dying from an overdose; but he was my friend.

To further supplement my income I began breaking more frequently into commercial premises. For example, I burgled a local bakery called the "Roly Poly" on Cowell Street. Most shops only yielded some petty cash, but I had to get money wherever I could find it. I knew that the bakery had no alarm system, so I just kicked in the bottom panel of the door and crawled through into the shop. I found some petty cash and some bags of coins ready for taking to the bank. As I turned to leave the shop, from the outside a torch shone through onto my face. My first thought was that it must be a policeman. As the torch moved a little to one side, I could see that it was a man in civilian dress, so I thought that he couldn't be a policeman. It could have been the proprietor for all I knew. Pondering what to do about this unexpected situation, I decided that the only thing was to intimidate this man and frighten him into standing back. I thought that I had the upper hand, since he didn't know who was inside, if there was more than one, or how big I was. I was coming out of the darkness, which is intimidating. Usually, burglars who are disturbed avoid confrontation and run away as quick as they can, but this man was blocking my escape route.

I started yelling and swearing at the man to get out of my way or I would kill him. He stood to one side and I thought the aggression had worked and I began running down the street, a little awkwardly because of the bags of coins in my hands. Glancing back I noticed that the man was running after me, which was really annoying. Then I noticed another man in front, walking towards me. My first thought was that this person was on his way home after a late night at a club or something. But as I changed direction a little to avoid him, he changed too, to intercept me. Suddenly I knew what was going on.

Both these men were CID and were in communication by radio. It was a trap and I was right in it. I still wasn't too worried, I was a good runner, I had the momentum of speed and he was just walking. Head down, I would just run straight through him as if he wasn't there. I would knock him flying. I'm like a rugby player heading for the line and nothing is going to stop me. Plus, I would meet him with the sole of my trainer to his chest, a well-timed kick would brush him aside. However, this man must have been something of a rugby player too, because a split second before I lifted my foot, he sprang forward and expertly tackled me around the waist. I came crashing to the ground and banged my head on the pavement. I think he rather enjoyed our brief encounter, at least, that's how he would probably tell it to his mates in the pub. The next thing I knew, he was kneeling on my back and I was being handcuffed with both policemen over me. I was off to the Police Station to be charged. At the Police Station I was charged and the usual process of taking other offences into account was laboriously detailed and matched with reported crimes. Again I found myself back in court.

Chapter 7

Third time loser

After my first remand in Swansea I was sentenced to a term of community service, but once back on the streets of Llanelli, my life of crime and drugs had continued on a downward spiral. The burglary at the Roly Poly was the incident that brought me back to court, but numerous other offences combined with my absence from the community service all counted against me. I was remanded back to Swansea to await reports before sentencing. Returning through the big steel gates of HMP Swansea would not be the same intimidating experience as before. I knew what I was facing and I knew how to cope with it. This time the outward bravado would be a little more real. My place in the pecking order of the youth wing would be virtually guaranteed.

It was a short remand, not much more than two months. This time the sentence handed down by the chairman of the magistrates was a two-year probation order. A community service order was obviously not going to work on me because we all knew I wouldn't turn up. The probation order may seem a soft sentence, but it had a purpose. Everyone knew that it would not be any deterrent to my criminal activities and I would eventually be back in court. Then, breaking my probation *and* committing further offences would all build up to a prison sentence. Once again, I was being given enough rope to hang myself.

I inevitably committed numerous offences while on probation. When I was arrested again for the usual catalogue of offences, this was all the ammunition the custody sergeant needed to convey down the line the message that this time I should receive a custodial sentence. As usual, Steve came to see me, armed with his cigarettes. He was honest with me. "Rich, if you get less than twelve months, it will be a bonus." He had been observing my growing career into more serious crime and the inevitable spells in jail. He had seen it all before. I was one of a breed whom he would expect to spend a substantial part of their life in prison or die of an overdose – so often the latter.

Once in the court, I found myself feeling nervous. Although prison no longer held any fear for me, this was different. I had come to the court from remand in the young offender's wing at Swansea and this time I knew the likely result would be a regular prison sentence. This was not going to be a community service order or more probation. I was thinking to myself, *"Oh no, I'm actually going to be doing proper bird this time, the real thing."* I pleaded guilty to everything and after a period of consultation between the chairman of the magistrates and the clerk of the court, the sentences for each of the offences were read out. Now apprehension turned to panic. I couldn't follow what they were saying. All I heard was two months for this, four months for that, six months for another. On and on the list ran. I was trying to keep count of the months and they were adding up to over two years! They were using the terms "concurrently" and "consecutively" over and over and I didn't know what the words meant. I thought, *"This sounds far too much, I haven't been that bad."* Alarmed, I looked at Steve and asked him what was going on. He said, "Don't worry Rich, I'll explain it all later, it's not all those months." Later I was relieved to discover that it all worked out to eight months. With remission for good behaviour, I would only do four months, not a bad result.

Back at Swansea I was sharing a cell with my mate Gringo. He was a little older than I was and serving a longer sentence. Being older than I was, Gringo had done time before so he knew the system. He said, "Listen Taylor, you can request where you want to go. Say it's easier for your family to visit. You should put down for Eastwood Park. It's brilliant there, you'll love it, man." He had been there before so he knew all about it. "Eastwood Park is easy Taylor, let's both put in for it and we'll go there together." "Okay Gringo, if it's easy like you say, let's go for it and see what happens."

One afternoon, a young officer named Williams came to the cell. "All right lads, pack your stuff, you're off tomorrow morning." "Where to boss?" "You're going to Eastwood Park." Very little warning, no time to make a phone call to your family, you're off. The next day we went to reception where we were given our plastic bags containing our personal possessions back. We stripped out of the prison uniform and dressed in our own clothes for the journey. The clothes had not been washed. After the formalities we were handcuffed for the journey in the meat wagon.

As we approached HMP Eastwood Park the thing that hit me first was the fence. I was expecting a high wall like Swansea. I stared in amazement at a razor wire fence. This makes a big difference to the atmosphere. You can see through a wire fence, the outside world is not completely cut off; it's visible whenever you care to look in that direction. It made a big difference to me. This was a lower category prison than Swansea, not so secure. Because I had a relatively short sentence and Gringo was coming towards the end of his, we were allocated to the lower category. Gringo's knowledge of the system was coming in handy. Eastwood Park was more modern and had no Victorian-style wings. The buildings were spaced better. We even had a key to our cells, which we kept on some string round our necks. We locked ourselves in at night.

As with other prisons, the first week was induction. This is the time when you learn their system, rules and regulations. During my induction week I was given the job of scrubbing floors. Hours of hard, boring and unpleasant work, on my knees with a large scrubbing brush held with both hands cleaning the tiles. If this wasn't bad enough, there were a number of female screws that were very unpleasant to us. One sticks out in my memory as being a rather butch woman who wore sensible shoes and had spiky hair. They took a perverse delight in antagonising young prisoners. "Slags" they called us. When one of them walked past the place where I was scrubbing, they would deliberately make a black scuff mark with their shoes on the tiles I had cleaned. Whenever this happened, it was tempting to give them a load of abuse. However, I managed to keep quiet and ignore the provocation. To say anything would mean being nicked and resulting in the loss of a couple of days remission. After induction week I had to apply for a job somewhere in the prison system. There were various options such as the kitchens, laundry or gardens. I applied for the kitchens, thinking that I would probably be able to get hold of extra food.

This prison used to be a borstal and it was old school. It retained the military discipline style of that kind of institution and even some of the former staff. The regime in prisons is very much determined by the governor and the senior staff. Our routine first thing in the morning was to clean and tidy our cell and bedding. The tiled floor had to be polished every day. My way of coping with this was to really get into it and see how shiny I could make my tiles. I even stole a spare towel as an addition to the polishing mop, which gave that extra bit of shine to my tiles. The liquid polish was applied with a cloth, then it was buffed until it gleamed. This left traces of powder from the dried polish that had to be carefully dusted off, not marking the amazing shine that I had so skilfully produced. The tiles looked magnificent and the officer inspecting was always impressed. I could have done a television advert for "Flash" in my cell. I was in competition with Gringo in the next cell. "My floor is more shiny than yours, Gringo." "Taylor, you're right off it man, anyone can see mine is shinier than yours. Anyway, you're cheating with that extra towel of yours." In a prison regime that is boring for most of the time, this sort of thing added a little fun and interest to the day.

Then, on the officer's command, we would step out of our cells and line up with our wash gear to file down to the toilet and wash area. We didn't march as such, but it was close, very regimented. For many prisoners, this regimentation helped them do their bird. You didn't have to make a decision, take any responsibility or show any initiative. You were just told what to do and when to do it – easy. There are a few old lags that actually prefer life inside. Three meals a day, a roof and a bed, television in the evening and a bit of pocket money for their cigarettes. Better than living

on the streets, which for some was the alternative. After
returning our morning wash gear to the cell, at last it was
down to the canteen for breakfast. The food was reasonable,
especially for me, because I ate very little when I was outside
on drugs.

The kitchen was run by a couple of civilians who were
professional chefs. Three or four prisoners helped them. I was
assigned to the "coppers". These were three large boilers that
cooked anything that consisted of a powder mixed with
boiling water. My work involved filling, mixing, getting it
exactly to right temperature and then pouring out. Tipping
out the contents into other containers required strength and
care. I took pride in doing my job exactly right. Curry,
custard, tea, coffee, soup and sauces, these were my domain
and I took pride in making them just right. Five or six
hundred hungry men had to be fed three times a day in three
servings and I was a vital part of this big operation. Everything had to be spotless. In fact the whole prison was clean in
comparison to Swansea, which was dirty.

One unusual thing about my time in Eastwood Park was
that I never once went outside. Exercise was inside in the
gym once a week. The gym instructor didn't like me for some
reason and used to make me work very hard until I was
exhausted. Perhaps it was because everyone called me Taffy
and maybe he didn't like Welshmen. I envied those that had
chosen outside work. My job had its own perks though. I was
able to steal bits of food that I enjoyed, such as jam, cheese or
ham and take it back to my cell. We were frisked before
leaving the kitchen, but by wrapping the stuff in cling film
and stuffing it down our pants, we could get it out. Or we
would go to the toilet and hide stuff there and return for it
later during association. A great luxury for me was milk. Any

chance I had while I was in the kitchen, I would drink milk while no one was looking.

The prison had a chapel with weekly services. I sometimes went to these, not because I was particularly interested in religion, but I did feel that it was a place of refuge. It was somewhere away from the rest of the regime, even though it was still inside the prison. Prisoners attended chapel services for a variety of reasons other than interest in any religion. They welcomed a change of routine or just seeing someone from the outside. I can remember that occasionally Christian groups from some local churches would come in and put on a special service with modern music and people telling the story of their conversion to Christianity. I would go if I was feeling bored. The chaplain was Church of England, but if anyone was Catholic or any other denomination or religion, they could request a minister of that religion to come in and visit them.

The drugs situation in Eastwood Park was very different from Swansea Young Offenders wing. Here the drugs were fewer and less obvious. Gringo had visitors who brought him drugs and he shared them with me. I was less dependent on drugs because I had more freedom of movement and I worked hard every day. My mind was more occupied, there was television and longer association. Back in Swansea where everyone was banged up twenty-three hours a day there was nothing else to think about. Taking drugs, scheming how to get hold of them and the dealing all helped to take away the boredom and gave everyone a purpose. The routine and strict discipline of Eastwood Park took away much of the mental vacuum. I didn't think these things through at the time, but looking back I can see how much better the regime was at Eastwood Park. I was always on the lookout for drugs, but

the kitchen work meant that I was up and out before
everyone else for food preparation and cleaning up after took
time, so I arrived back at my cell tired and ready for a kip.

It was while I was in Eastwood Park that, for the first time,
I began to think that I needed to sort myself out. But I didn't
know how to do it. Alone in my cell, I wondered what life
was all about and why was I here. What is the point of it all?
Not finding any answer, I pushed the questions to the back of
my mind, but the questions returned. I just didn't know what
to do about them.

Chapter 8

Usk Open

After three months, Gringo's past experience became useful again. He said, "Taylor, now we have been here three months, we can apply for transfer to open prison." I had never heard of open prison.

"Gringo, what are you talking about, man?" I asked.

"Look, because we are coming to the end of our time and we've behaved ourselves, we can probably get open prison for the rest," he informed me.

"What's it like, Gringo?"

"Taylor, you will love it man; it's a party. The place is called Usk Open, it's near Abergevenny. You can get booze, drugs are easier, all sorts of stuff, it's wild."

"Are you serious?"

"Yes, c'mon let's apply."

Gringo asked for the forms and we filled them in. A week later one of the officers came with the results of the application. "Okay lads, that's it, you're going next week." Gringo was really excited. I was too, but not as much as he, because I didn't yet know what it was like at Usk Open. "Yeah Taylor, we got it made, we're going to Usk, you're gonna really love it, man."

For the transfer we were handcuffed before we went into the van and all the way to Usk – this is normal for the transfer of prisoners. As we approached Usk Open, I had my first view of a whole different world as far as prisons are concerned. From the outside it looked like a country park. It had no walls, not even a fence. I couldn't believe it. Then even more of a surprise, as the barrier lifted for the van to enter, the officer said, "C'mon then lads, let's have the cuffs off" and our handcuffs were removed. Previously, whenever the police or prison officers had moved me around, I was always handcuffed. There I was in the back of a van and the cuffs were being removed; I just couldn't work it out at all. Gringo kept looking at me with an expression that said, *"I told you it was great."* As we drove down the drive I was getting excited too. The accommodation was a series of dormitories that looked like cabins. I couldn't see any bars on the windows. It resembled a rural army barracks.

As we stepped out of the van, I asked Gringo, "What's happening, man?" "Rich, I told you, it's open prison, you can just go if you want. People abscond all the time." Instead of fences or walls, there are boundaries that you must not cross. You are in trouble if you do and someone sees you. Having done three months, I could be out in just one more month if I retained my maximum remission, it would be easy. Again I had my own room and key. Induction week was cleaning floors again until you applied for work in a particular area. I applied for estate work which would give me the outside environment that I wanted. I put up fences or worked on the farm.

After settling into my room, I went for a walk round the site. I thought, *"I can go anywhere I like and no one is telling me what to do."* This freedom actually made it harder for me.

Like many other prisoners, I found the lack of restrictions or instructions difficult to cope with. This may seem strange, but all my life I had a history of going wild whenever I had no control or discipline. I certainly hadn't learned the art of self-discipline. In a closed prison there were no real decisions to make. An officer told you what to do, where to go and when to eat or sleep. In this place, I was responsible for locking my own door at night. There was a night curfew, but it was largely unmonitored. When not working, I was free to roam the grounds, visit any of the dorms and have a chat with anyone I liked. It felt very strange. Supervision by the officers was relaxed. They tended to walk around the site, generally observing the situation. They might walk the perimeter of the site, but anyone who wanted to go outside could easily dodge them. The prisoners were trusted not to abscond. Some did, but the majority had the motivation to complete their sentence in a regime that was as free as it could be while still being called a prison. If you were caught outside the perimeter, that was it, you were immediately transferred back to a closed prison.

Some of the officers would hide around the perimeter and try to catch anyone who absconded. They knew that prisoners went over the line, mostly for a short time at night to get supplies of booze or drugs. It was a game that both sides played. For me it was a disaster, because I went wild. I used the freedom to the hilt. I arranged for my dad to bring deliveries of booze to a drop near the prison. At night I would sneak out and collect it. I learned how to do this from other prisoners. The first time, I went out with someone else to help bring in a stash that had been left at the drop by their family. It was easy. I would write to my dad and tell him the exact place to drop stuff and when. It may have been behind a hedge, opposite a road sign, in a country lane a few minutes run across the fields from the perimeter. Running across fields in the dark wasn't easy, but it was part of the challenge and adrenalin drove us on. There were certain places, easy to identify, that were known drops. On other occasions, I would go out to known drops in search of other people's stashes and pinch them. Sometimes I could listen in on someone's phone call when they were arranging a drop and then go with a friend from Llanelli, run to the drop before them, and return to the prison a different way. Gringo had gone; he managed to keep his remission, which was the original plan. I had completely lost the plot.

After a drop, I really started packing. I was drinking, taking tablets and smoking drugs. Consequently I was off my face a lot of the time. My behaviour deteriorated. I became abusive and all normal judgement was gone as in the past in Llanelli. I began breaking the rules. I was not getting up in the morning for work because I was still plastered. I was caught out of my room at night and nicked. This resulted in some of my four months remission being withdrawn. At other times I became involved in fights and lost more days remission. An officer involved in the estate work might tell me to do something and I would tell him to "F" off. He would say, "Okay, two days remission lost." That was the punishment. In the end I lost about sixty days remission. My supposed one month in Usk Open stretched to three. Instead of four months in prison, I did a total of six.

After I came home from Usk, it seemed to me that I kept bumping into people who told me that they had become Christians. I wasn't sure what they meant, but something had happened to them. Some of them were mates and I knew them as addicts or alcoholics, but here they were telling me about God and telling me how my life too could be changed like theirs. This really did my head in and I tried to steer clear of them. Yet I kept meeting them as I walked around town. One Saturday I was in town with Bunch and there were some people giving out Christian leaflets and inviting people to some meeting. We met one of them whose nickname was "Gok". I don't know how he had such a nickname; his real name is Allen Andrews. Today he runs a rehabilitation place for addicts in Llanelli called "Choose Life". He didn't hold back, "C'mon boys, give up the drugs and turn to Jesus. Jesus loves you too. I did and it's great." That's how he talked to us, no embarrassment. He was bold. I thought, *"He's right off it, the drugs have snapped him."* If this was religion, it was very different from the quiet version I saw at the prison chapel. This guy was on the street telling everyone about it.

Then Bunch and I were invited to go to a church meeting in a big old hall in Lakefield Road. It was a church called Antioch. The pastor was a woman named Karen Lowe. We went on a Sunday night, just for a laugh. We were absolutely hammered drunk. We staggered in and slumped down in the back row. When the singing began we sang louder than anyone else. We were just mocking the whole proceedings. For us it was one big laugh. Anyone who testified to their faith in God, we just laughed at them; it was cruel. I was thinking, *"What idiots, Christianity is a load of crap."* We talked during the preaching, but the preacher continued in spite of the distraction. At the end of the sermon, he asked if anyone wanted to be a Christian. If they did, they should come to the front and he would pray for them. People were going to the front and a guy prayed for them. Some fell to the floor as they were prayed for. This intrigued me. I was sure it was fake, he must be pushing them over. I wanted to know if

it was real so I said to Bunch, "C'mon, let's go to the front."
I was so drunk that it would be a miracle if I stayed standing
up.

We staggered to the front and the man asked us to kneel
down. Perhaps he too realised that we might fall over. We
kneeled down and he put his hand on my head. I immediately
felt a strange warmth flow through my body, from my head
down. What happened next was the strangest thing that had
ever happened to me – I was instantly stone cold sober;
Bunch too. After the initial shock, my reaction was one of
anger. This guy had got one over me. He had something I
didn't understand. Plus, I had spent a lot of money getting as
drunk as I was and now it was all a waste. I stood up and
stormed out, walking in a very straight line. Angry though I
was, the experience had totally freaked me out and I was
scared; I couldn't explain it.

This was the first time I had encountered anything that I
would call spiritual power. Again I pushed things to the back
of my mind and tried to ignore it. I never went back to the
church again. I was afraid the same might happen and I
wanted to stay as I was. I didn't want to be cured, healed,
blessed, saved or anything else they might have for me. I
continued to bump into people, especially mates, who had
been converted to Christianity. Apart from Gok, there was
Colin Lloyd, Nigel Haddock and Harty, who had been one of
the biggest drug addicts in Llanelli. Everyone knew him. He
totally changed and it was obvious that whatever had
happened to him was powerful stuff. There was nothing
polished about them, no religious jargon, they just expressed
what they felt. "Taylor, give your heart to Jesus, man, He'll
sort your head out." They were totally raw, but there was a
power and a freshness that was hard to deny. Bunch started to

get into it and began going to some of their house meetings. I nearly went with him, after all Bunch and I were inseparable. In the end, I didn't go. "No Bunch, you run off, I don't want to know." I was afraid of losing my lifestyle and having nothing to replace it with. All this happened about a week after coming home from Usk Open. Bunch never made it through to a solid faith, he too found the change far too great. A couple of weeks later we were back on the booze and drugs as bad as we ever were.

Chapter 9

Sinking lower

By now I had become a very nasty piece of work. I was aggressive and obnoxious to almost anyone I met. The world that enclosed me was a prison of my own making. Anything outside it wasn't worth my attention. My only loyalty was to my need for drugs. Bunch was my mate, but even this relationship was based on our partnership in crime and drugs, which suited us both. One job we did together was in Andrews Street and was destined to have far more serious consequences than either of us could have imagined. I had, by now, just turned eighteen. We were walking from town back to Bunch's house to drink. All day we had been taking a cocktail of tablets, smoking ganja and drinking. When I was high on tablets, I was always looking to do jobs; the drugs had the effect of making me feel invincible. My judgement was completely screwed. In this frame of mind, we were walking the back lanes and I was looking for an opportunity, ready for anything. This was true of me, but not Bunch. Even though he was older than I was, I usually took the initiative.

I chose a house, more or less at random, climbed over the back gate and approached the door. I hadn't checked to see if anyone was at home first – which was the normal and necessary procedure. The effect of the drugs took away any fear. I tried the back door and it was open. Not even this made me cautious, I just walked boldly in, oblivious of consequences. Entering the lounge, I saw the television on, gas fire alight, slippers and cigarettes beside it, just as if someone had popped out or was even upstairs. I grabbed the cigarettes and some jewellery. I told Bunch to spin the upstairs and I would continue downstairs. I thought that if the occupant came back, I would be nearest the back door to escape. It would be Bunch that was caught. Bunch said, "I'm not going up there, you're right off it Taylor, you go up," so I said to him, "If you hear *anything*, you shout 'It's on top, it's on top', all right?" This was a phrase we used as a warning when trouble was imminent. "All right, Taylor." I ran upstairs and began to spin the bedrooms where I found some jewellery. As I came down, I heard a key turn in the door. I felt a sudden rush. Should I go back upstairs and hide under the bed, or should I face this person, whoever it might be? That it could be anyone, a bouncer from a nightclub, or more than one person, flashed through my mind. I dashed past the opening door into the lounge.

It was a mother and daughter. The daughter saw me first. "Mammy, there's someone in the house," she yelled. The mother pushed past and began screeching obscenities at us. Her yelling was fuelled more by fear than anger. We ran out, over the gate, down the back lane and into the main road. The route would take us over the road, down another alley, past the Salvation Army place beside the river, leading to Felinfoel, where Bunch lived. She came back out the front door into the street, yelling, "Stop them, they've burgled my house." There were quite a lot of people around to hear her in this residential street. The woman was chasing us and a man with a walking stick was coming towards us, cutting off our escape. I don't know how much he needed this aid, because he was running and waving the stick in the air. I was dropping some of the jewellery and the rest I threw into the river, intending to try to retrieve it later. I was ahead of Bunch and managed to swerve round the man in classic rugby fashion. Bunch however, met him head on. The man was fairly large, well armed with his stick and very aggressive. I looked back to see that he had brought Bunch down and was beating him furiously with the stick. In fact, Bunch later brought an assault complaint against the man. The police wouldn't co-operate and the complaint was never followed through. Bunch yelled, "Taylor, help me." I ran back and grabbed the man and threw him to one side with strength fuelled by adrenalin and drugs. Bunch jumped up and we were off.

Unfortunately, the walking stick man lived in the same area as Bunch and knew his face. He knew my face also, because I had seen him from time to time in the market. A few hours later we were arrested on suspicion of aggravated burglary. This is a much more serious charge than ordinary burglary. It was "aggravated" because the householder had come home while we were still inside. The fright and stress this causes the victim makes it a much more serious charge. Later, after I had been drinking in the Denever, two cops were waiting for me as I came out. Bunch had already been detained and I was convinced that he would grass me up. Witnesses identified us later in separate line-ups. Worryingly, this charge would probably mean a much longer sentence.

We knew pretty well the course that events would now take. We appeared in the magistrates' court merely to be remanded in Swansea. The magistrates would pass us on to the Crown Court, which had the power to send us down for a much longer stretch. While we were waiting in the cells below the magistrates' court, a strange incident happened.

Drug addicts will try taking anything that they think will sort them out, even if they are not sure what it is, or its effect. Bunch and I were in the same cell below the magistrates court, waiting our turn. I had rung Mammy and told her we needed stuff and to bring whatever she could get. She brought six tablets and smuggled them into the toilets below the court. Neither of us recognised the tablets – and we knew a thing or two about tablets. "Mammy, what on earth are these?" "I don't know Rich, they were all I could get quickly. I was told they're all right." I asked Bunch, "What shall we do with them?" He said, "Let's do 'em." "But we don't know what they are. Let's take one and if they are any good, we can take the rest." Bunch wasn't having any of it, "No, let's do the lot." We took three each.

After that, I remember walking up to the dock, but nothing more. I was just gone. When I woke up, I hadn't a clue where I was or how long I had been out. I was wearing blue pyjamas, lying in a bed that had the top sheet sewn to the mattress – I guess to prevent the likes of me falling out. Looking round, I was obviously in a cell somewhere, which, apart from the bed, was empty. My first thought was that I had been sectioned for being off my head. After wriggling out of the sheets, I started yelling and kicking the door, demanding to know where I was. My yelling wasn't up to my usual Police Station standard because my mouth was incredibly dry. I think I was more afraid than angry. *"Why am I here? Do they think I'm mad? Will they let me out?"*

A female officer came and told me that I was in the hospital wing of HMP Swansea. She had no details to explain why I was there or what had happened to me; she had just come on duty. There was no charge sheet and no medical information because the incident had happened outside the prison. She also told me that she couldn't let me out, she wasn't even allowed to open the door. I explained that I was very thirsty and must have a drink. I couldn't get out for one until the next morning at slop-out time. I was desperate. She brought water but the door only had a small peephole with a flap, not even large enough to pass a small cup through. She tried her best to pour the water through the hole, and I opened my mouth under the trickle of water. It was a crazy situation, but it was all she could do for me without further instructions. I was glad of even that small amount of water.

Stephen Lloyd came to see me a week later and said, "You must be mad, Rich. There I was, trying to represent you to the magistrates and you were yelling and swearing at them." "What do you mean?" I said. "Rich, you were yelling at me saying 'Go on Steve, you tell 'em Steve, tell 'em I'm a good bloke.'" I couldn't remember any of it. When I went back on the wing, I was lying on my bed and hearing my mother's voice saying, *"Richard, come on, your dinner's on the table."* I jumped up and looked around to see if she was there. I said to my cellmate, "Did you hear my mother?" He must have thought I was mad. The tablets were still messing my head up.

My cell overlooked the exercise yard and I heard Bunch calling up to my window. This time it wasn't my head playing tricks; I looked out and he was on exercise. "Taylor, them tablets your Mammy gave us were right off it, man. I've been in hospital for three days." "And I have," I replied. "I keep hearing voices," Bunch complained. "So do I," I said and we both had a good laugh. Once fully recovered, we had our half-hour in court, this time without the funny tablets.

For me, the remand in Swansea turned out to be for six months. I had committed numerous burglaries, but the more serious offence of aggravated burglary was the key to the future sentence. The offences had been committed while I was on police bail – this also made matters worse. It all added up to the possibility of a stretch of four or five years. The magistrates remanded us to await appearance in the Crown Court for sentencing. I was still young enough for the young offender's section, but Bunch was older and he went to the adult section, which was "A" wing. During the remand, I appeared in court for other offences and my remand was therefore lengthened so that all the offences could be taken into account in one court appearance. It was 1 April 1993, and I was the fool who had refused to learn anything from past mistakes.

Chapter 10

Looking for answers

During the six months on remand I began to ask questions of myself. Soul-searching questions. *"Why am I here? What is going on with me? What is life all about? Why am I so messed up?"* All my younger brothers were following the same path as I was; I felt responsible and guilty about it. They were messed up on drugs and I thought that if I had set a better example they might not be in the same mess as I was. I had taken them with me to commit crimes and introduced them to criminal activities. It wasn't just my family, there were many others I had led astray and totally messed up their lives. Some even died later of drugs overdoses. All this began to weigh on my conscience for the first time. Even today I still feel troubled when I think back to the people, events and places that lie deep in my memory. I can't change the past, it is something I have to live with, to try to overcome the depressing memories and live above them. While on the wing, I resumed all the same activities of wheeling and dealing drugs. I was an accomplished trader, well established, high up the pecking order. I was *the man*.

To help me cope with my feelings of guilt I began to attend

the chapel in the prison. Both Church of England and
Catholic services were held there. I went to the Church of
England services. The minister was Ted Hunt, a very tall man
whose warmth and friendliness matched his height. I felt
comfortable in his presence. Ted would tell us stories about
Jesus who forgave prostitutes and sinners like me. I liked the
stories, but the experience was much more than that. I felt
really good when I was in Chapel. It was a comfortable refuge
for me from everything else in the prison. Here I could take
off the mask, just be myself and relax. I didn't have to be
Taylor the hard man, living by his wits, hassling everyone and
generally playing the part that I felt was necessary for me if I
was to do my bird on my own terms. Whenever they served
communion it had a remarkable effect on me. I felt somehow
clean. As I took the bread and wine a strange warm feeling
went through my body and I didn't understand it. This wasn't
just because it was real wine. Some prisoners would try to
take a much bigger gulp of wine than was intended and this
would result in a bit of a tugging match for the cup with the
Verger. This experience may not fit in with a lot of people's
theology, but God used these communion times to speak to
me. All I can say is, I believe I was experiencing the presence
of God for the first time.

This strange feeling unsettled me. I didn't mind a bit of
religion, which made me feel better, but this was too close to
home; too personal. I tried to push it to the back of my mind.
I didn't want anything intruding on the inner me. As far as I
was concerned this was a no-go area. Yet I still wanted
answers to life – but answers that didn't include God.

During these five months, I had visits from a few friends
who had become Christians and wanted to tell me all about
it. One of these was Colin Lloyd, who had done stuff with me

and was an alcoholic. I listened but wouldn't let on that I was in any way interested. Then I had a visit from a worker with "Prison Fellowship" named Ken Shingleton. This excellent organisation exists to help prisoners and share the Gospel of Christ with them. He was a Methodist "Local Preacher". Ken was a counsellor and although I was not sure what that meant, he sounded like the sort of person I should talk to.

To my surprise, after I told Ken what my problem was, he started telling me about his own life and the difference that God had made. He had a completely different background and experience from me. No drugs or crime, just an ordinary bloke. However, that didn't matter, he still made a big impression on me. He was totally genuine and real. This came across so strongly; it impacted me more than anything he said. He had worked all his life, cared for his family and paid his taxes. Yet here he was, listening to the likes of me. All I had done in life was to take, take, take, to hurt and destroy other people's lives. I just couldn't work it out.

In Ken I saw genuine concern and compassion that wasn't tied to any conditions. I had never seen this before. I asked Ken if he would come and see me again and he answered, "I'll come again next week." Then he began to tell me about Jesus and how He loved me. He kept telling me that God had a plan for my life. To my embarrassment, tears began to roll down my cheeks. I hadn't cried for years; I hardened myself to such emotions. I needed to maintain my reputation for hardness in the young offenders wing and here I was crying. I thought, *"What's happening to me?"* I wiped my face and tried to pull myself together. I asked him, "Can this God change my life? Does He care about me? Will Jesus forgive my sins? Can He turn my life around?" Ken said, "He'll do it for you too, Richard; all you have to do is talk to Him and ask Him."

I still couldn't stop the tears. I was all messed up emotionally. He offered me a Bible, but I told him I had one already in my cell. Every cell has a Bible supplied by the "Gideons" organisation which places them in millions of hotels, prisons, hospitals and schools all over the world.

I went back to my cell thinking hard about Ken's words. They had made an enormous impact on me. My cellmate had gone to the gym and I was left alone with my thoughts. I sat on my bunk, looking out of my window, staring at the view. I could see the Swansea council buildings and even though it was a misty day, I could just see the Mumbles in the distance. Then for the first time, I talked to God. I simply said, "God, if You're there, change my life." At that moment, something changed inside me. I connected with something. This is the only way I can explain the experience. There I was, eighteen years old, a heroin addict in prison and this layman with a heart for messed-up people had spoken the words that brought me to God in some way. Not many outside his family and friends have ever heard of Ken; he has never stood on a great stage or appeared on television, yet he was the vital link in the chain of events that had brought me to this place. Ken was a humble, unassuming, middle-aged guy, dressed in a tweed jacket with a brown tie and the sort of person I would have arrogantly dismissed as a "muppet". Later I visited Ken and his wife Sheila in their home. I thanked God for sending such a lovely man to tell me the things I needed to know. During the remaining weeks on remand, Ken visited me almost weekly and shared with me the basics of the Christian faith.

The Bibles in our cells had nice thin pages, so if we were out of cigarette paper we would tear out pages and use them to roll our cigarettes. Shortly after my first prayer, I needed some paper for my cigarette. I opened the Bible randomly and tore out a page and did myself a roll-up. I struck the match, but suddenly, I found that I had an inner voice that I wasn't used to hearing. It said, *"This is all wrong, I shouldn't be doing this to a page from the Bible. I should be reading this, not putting a match to it."* I blew the match out, unrolled the page, and began to read it. It was the Gospel of John, chapter 1. I read the page and then read most of that Gospel, about twenty chapters, before I put it down. I found it captivating. I was lying on my bunk with the Bible resting on my chest and fell asleep. Sleeping in prison is not easy because of the noise and I wasn't on any drugs – my usual way of drifting off to sleep. Nevertheless, I slept the deepest and most peaceful sleep that I could remember. From early afternoon, right through to the next morning, I slept. It was as if the weariness of years of turmoil, crime, drugs, aggression and fighting was being rolled away through peaceful sleep. My subconscious mind was being cleared of the nightmares of my life up to now. The Bible talks about the peace of God that passes anyone's understanding and perhaps this was my first experience of it.

The next day I read more and the more I read the Bible, the more I wanted to know about this man called Jesus. I went to Chapel every Sunday and wanted to be involved. I still wasn't sure if I was a Christian yet or not, I just wanted to know more about God. I asked Ted if I could help in any way with the Chapel services. I just wanted to take part somehow. He agreed to let me help with the incense. In Catholic and high Church of England services, incense is lit in a small container suspended by a chain. This is then swung from side to side to spread the smoke and smell around as the procession of those taking part in the service walks down to the front of the church. I was keen to do anything, so I agreed. I thought that by taking part, I would get closer to God. I was shown how to prepare the incense and to put on all the special white robes for the job. I looked a real idiot in them. If any of my mates saw me they would collapse laughing. But I didn't care.

On the first Sunday I took part I went early to the vestry, got all dressed up in the robes and lit the incense. I had to walk to the front of the church and make the sign of the cross with the incense. Then I turned to the altar to do it again, before turning to the congregation to repeat the same thing. Some of my mates were in church and they had a really good laugh at my expense. In my robes, swinging the incense, I was the funniest thing they had seen for a long time. "Taylor, you are right off it, man." But I wasn't embarrassed by it; I didn't care what they thought about me. One week, Ken brought a guy who sang and played the guitar. He didn't sing a Christian song, he sang the group U2's hit song, "I still haven't found what I'm looking for". This really connected with me. My heart cried out that this was me, I too was looking for something. He then told his own story of how he became a Christian and had been "born again".

Back in my cell, I still regularly smoked cannabis, but I also read the Bible every night for the remainder of my remand. Something was happening to me, because my addiction began to lessen and the amount of drugs I smoked reduced as a consequence. I was still in the drug-obsessed environment of the wing, but I now had an alternative focus to the drugs. The Bible reading, going to Chapel, praying, all was beginning to change me, without me noticing at first. My foul language began to moderate. I was accustomed to include swear words in almost every sentence, but this lessened as the weeks passed, until it stopped altogether. My attitude changed. I had always been very aggressive, very unpleasant, and the screws, understandably, didn't like me. In an establishment full of undesirables, I stood out to them as particularly obnoxious. I also read a book from the prison library that influenced me called *Tell it to the Mafia* by Joe Donato [1] He had been a Mafia member before becoming a Christian. There were many parallels between his life and mine. It really spoke to me. I realised that if God could change him, He could change me too.

My prayers were not the standard type, they were more a series of questions that I would ask God, especially about things I read in the Bible. I gradually adopted a state of mind where I was carrying on a debate with myself. I was trying to convince myself that God existed and the Bible was true. I extended this debate by trying to convince other prisoners. I would go to my fellow inmates during association with my Bible in hand (I now had a new one) and debate with them. I would often have a group around me listening and putting counter-arguments. "Listen guys, look out of your cell window at the trees and the sky. Someone must have made all that. Look here in the Bible. It says, 'In the beginning God created the heavens and the earth'. Where else did it come from?" I was preaching to them, but convincing myself. My mates didn't know what to think. "That Taylor, he's got God now, he's right off it, man, the drugs have finally done him." My big reputation was now helpful because the guys were more inclined to listen. During association, instead of playing pool, I would have a group around me and I would read them stories from the Bible. Some even went back to their cells and read their own Bible as a result. I was a sort of evangelist,

even before I was properly a Christian. I was still taking
drugs.

Note

1. Joe Donato, *Tell it to the Mafia*, Logos International, 1975, ISBN
    088270107X.

Chapter 11

An unexpected miracle

Near the end of my five months, I was mopping the floor on the fours when Ted, the Chaplain, walked up.

"Taylor 791."

"Yes, boss?"

"I've got someone on the phone who wants to speak to you."

"Who is it, boss?" I asked, curious.

"It's a surprise, come down to my office."

We walked over to his office which was in "A" wing. His phone was off the hook and he picked it up and said, "Dinah, I've got this young man here now; I think he needs to come to your place because he needs help. He's a good lad, has great potential, but he needs to come to you." I hadn't a clue what was going on. I was soon up for sentencing, I was looking at five years; there was no way that I was getting out. *"What on earth is he talking about?"* I wondered. He said to me, "This is Dinah Sansome, she runs a place called Victory Outreach and she wants to speak to you. I know you are up for sentencing in a few weeks, but there is a chance we can get you in with Dinah." Unknown to me, Ted and Ken had been talking to Dinah about my situation. They had told her about my Bible reading and my participation in the services.

I picked up the phone and said, "Hello?" Dinah had the warmest, friendliest voice I had ever heard. "Hello Richard, I want you to come home," she said. I was puzzled. "What do you mean? I don't have a home." She continued, "I know, we want to be your family, will you come home?" I instantly became a wreck; I just started crying. It was twenty minutes of sobbing before I could compose myself. I asked, "What was all that about, Ted?"

"When you appear in court, Dinah, Ken and I will be there too," he said. "We will try to get sentencing deferred for a month pending further reports and we will see if you can be bailed to the hostel." Later, from my cell window, I shouted down to Bunch out on exercise. "Bunch, I don't know what's happening with all this God stuff, but something is going on inside me, man."

The meat wagon picked us up to take us to the Crown Court. We sat in the holding cells beneath in the usual way, waiting our turn. I was thinking about God and the Bible. I thought *"If there is a God, this is His chance to prove it to me."* This was an impossible situation. I had already had two applications for bail rejected and you are only allowed three. Virtually no one has their third application accepted. If I walked free from court that day, it would be a miracle.

The call came: "Taylor and Morgan, court one." An officer came, opened our door and put on our handcuffs. "C'mon lads, off we go." I had never been in a Crown Court before. As I gazed around, I could see that it was very different from the magistrates court. People were wearing wigs, there were posh barristers. The judge wore a red and black robe and peered at us over half-frame spectacles perched on the end of his nose. It was very intimidating. The effect was to convince me that this was serious. Many times I had bounced out of the magistrates court with a smirk on my face, but there was no smirking in this place. This was the real thing. "Sit down; thank you," snapped the judge. We sat down with everyone else. "Remain standing Taylor and Morgan," the judge said to us in a tone, that if I called it unfriendly, would be a massive understatement. We were up and ramrod straight in an instant. I was scared rigid. Any hope of a miracle was quickly fading from my mind. A barrister read out our names, our last known abode, and the charges against us. This complete, the judge said, "Sit down." I sank into my seat. I thought, *"This guy hates us, he is going to enjoy putting us away for a long time."* We were hoping for four years, but this judge could give us seven! I prayed silently.

Then a very strange thing happened. I felt a hand on my right shoulder. I turned to see who it was and was puzzled to see that no one was there. I assumed I must have imagined it, but when I turned back the hand – or at least the feeling of a hand – was still there. I looked again. The same thing. This was spooky. Furthermore, I could feel the warmth from the invisible hand coming through my clothes and into my body. I was freaked out. I thought it must have been an officer, but no one was near me. The hand had a dramatic effect on me. A sense of absolute assurance that everything was going to be all right came over me. Peace replaced dread in my mind.

I looked across the courtroom and I could see in the public seats a middle-aged woman with blonde hair smiling at me. This was Dinah, but I hadn't met her yet. I wondered who she was. She just kept smiling at me the whole time. Again, it was a smile that said, "Everything is going to be all right." I was thinking, *"Who is that woman?"* While we were in the

cells, my barrister asked me if there was anything that I
wanted him to say to the judge on my behalf. Some people
will say they are sorry and hope for a lesser sentence. I said,
"Well actually, there is. Please tell the judge that I have been
reading the Bible, going to church in prison and something is
beginning to happen to me. I don't know what it is, but I feel
as if I'm changing." This sort of statement would normally
cause some cynicism in a court, because all prisoners are liars.
However, my barrister said this to the judge, word for word
and with some sincerity. Plus, he added words of his own. He
talked as if I was already a Christian and mentioned how God
had changed my life. I was absolutely flabbergasted. What I
didn't know at the time, but found out to my amazement
much later, was that my barrister was a born-again Christian
and had actually believed what I told him.

Looking back later, I was amazed at the way God arranged
things for me on that day. My barrister asked if I could be
bailed to Victory Outreach for a month. He also drew
attention to Dinah's presence. "Your honour, we have a
representative from Victory Outreach in court today and
there is a letter of support from them in your notes." The
judge looked at his notes for a few moments and read the
letter. "Oh yes, Victory Outreach," he said, "I have heard
of them many times, they have represented people before.
Yes, excellent work, who is representing them today?"
Acknowledging his glance towards the public gallery, Dinah
lifted her hand a little and smiled her magic smile. "Fine, I
don't need to speak to her," the judge said. Then reverting
to his previous unfriendly tone, he spoke directly to us:
"Morgan and Taylor, stand up please." This was the moment
Bunch and I had been dreading. "Morgan, in your case, I
remand you for a further month pending sentencing, until

September 13th – take him away." At this my heart leapt; this meant that he was treating us separately. Before I could think, he continued, "Taylor, in your case, you are the younger of the two and I sense that you have been led astray by this Morgan." Of course, this just wasn't true; in fact it was the reverse. Later, Bunch was furious about these remarks. The judge continued, "I have listened to your barrister's thoughts today and a letter has been put before me. I'm going to give you a try. I think there is hope for you. I do believe that the Christian faith can bring a sense of value and change in a man or woman's life. I therefore bail you – with conditions – to Victory Outreach."

As I was escorted back to the cells to wait for processing my mind was in a spin, my emotions all jumbled. I didn't know whether to laugh or cry. I was certainly very excited about the opportunity that the judge had given me. I was thinking, *"I've just got out, I shouldn't be getting out, what's going on here?"* When the papers were complete, I gathered my things and said goodbye to Bunch, which was very difficult because he was on his way back to Swansea prison as I was on my way out. Bunch was going to do a stretch, mainly because of the Andrews Street job, which I dragged him into! I left the cells clutching my bag and went downstairs where I found three people waiting for me. Dinah was there, plus Jane from Prison Fellowship and Matthew Evans, a recovered drug addict. I was a free man!

They took me down to the cafeteria in the court building for a wonderful cup of tea (the tea I had been drinking for five months in Swansea prison was appalling). For me this was surreal. I was thinking, *"This is a dream, it can't be happening, I am going to wake up in a minute."* I tried to concentrate on what they were saying. They told me about Victory Outreach and began to list all the rules that they had, which were very strict. No television, no drinking or wearing earrings, the hours I was to keep, and many other measures designed to make the rehabilitation work. I immediately took out my earring and put it in the ashtray on the table. We went down to the car park and boarded their car for the journey to Victory Outreach. It had all happened so quickly, my mind was finding it difficult to catch up with one event before we moved on to the next. In the back of the car I sat in silence for the whole two and a half hour journey to Abertillery.

Chapter 12

Transformation

I had no idea what Victory Outreach would look like. I was surprised to discover, as we pulled into the drive, that it is housed in a former hotel called "The Bush Hotel", a big old building that fitted nicely into its surroundings on the edge of Abertillery town centre. Victory Outreach had not always been here. It began in the sixties in London, with Dinah taking food and clothes to drug addicts and others who were living on the streets. She then opened up her own home as a refuge for addicts. Later the Bishop of Gloucester arranged for her to have an old vicarage as a centre. Since then, the work has grown and they have about six centres around the country. I was feeling nervous, even though they tried to put me at ease, assuring me that there were others just like me, happily living there.

Still a bit bewildered, I was escorted inside and introduced to the staff, several of whom were former addicts. Everyone was very friendly and there was real warmth in the welcome. I sat in the office while they went through my details and one of the former addicts went through more of the rules with me, many of which I just couldn't understand at the time.

Apart from those I had been told about, no television or non-Christian music was allowed. Television was limited to the news and some sports programmes. They had a large library of Christian videos, most of which were preaching tapes. No girlfriends were allowed and part of our social security payment had to be paid in as rent. Smoking was allowed outside the building at certain times, but only if you were alone. Groups were not allowed to smoke together. We were not allowed visits or phone calls to or from friends and relatives for the first three months. No outside contact at all, which for me was very difficult. Being cut off from everyone and everything I had known took a lot of getting used to. The rules seemed at first to be over the top; later I could see that they were the result of long experience in this kind of work.

The daily timetable was very structured. Morning devotions started at 7.30am and lasted half an hour. There was singing and prayers followed by someone preaching a short sermon. The next hour was devoted to breakfast and our individual chores which were called "house jobs". Residents were allocated a room or area to clean each day. At 9.00am we began our "works programme". This consisted mainly of maintenance and improvement work on the building. If we had any experience or skills, such as electrical or carpentry work, these were utilised. The programme also gave us the opportunity to acquire various skills. With a building of this size and age, we never ran out of work. One time I was given the task of cleaning out the cellar, which was dirty and damp – a very unpleasant job. I kept thinking, *"What on earth am I doing here?"* At 10.30am they had another meeting, at 1.30pm, another meeting, and at 8.30pm, yet another meeting, all along the same pattern as the morning devotions! To my mind, it was a very weird regime.

I was shown to my room, which I shared with a guy called Ken Parker. He was Irish and had recently come from a place called Spike Island Prison. He was under the same remand conditions as I was. I suppose that I was put with him because he was just one step ahead of me. At night I would ask him questions about his experience. I unpacked my gear and stashed it in the wardrobe. Then I lay down on my bed for the rest of the afternoon. I was thinking that it was just another kind of open prison. This place had got me out of jail, but I didn't really want to be there, I wanted to go back to Llanelli. I found that I still looked at the place with my old dark instincts. *"Where do they keep the cash? Is there a safe? I could do a runner from here and be back in Llanelli in no time."* I was free, but I didn't feel free. For me, freedom was doing my own thing in Llanelli. Yet God had already done something in me that restrained me from taking this backward step to my previous life. The spooky experiences unnerved me, but drew me on. I had to see if the God I read about in the Bible, really did have a plan for my life. If He did, I wanted to know about it.

I went down to the dining room for my first meal with the rest of the lads. About twenty-five of us sat round a large table and much of the conversation was about how God was changing their lives. It was very interesting for me to hear their stories. "I was on heroin but God changed my life and now I am free," was a typical remark. Some people were introduced to me and they all seemed keen to tell me their story. After the meal I went out for a cigarette before returning to my room for a while. I read some of the letters I had received while in prison, still struggling with my doubts about the place. They had four meetings every day, with singing, prayer and preaching – attendance was compulsory.

This seemed totally over the top to me. I was used to going to church once a week.

At 8.30pm, I went down to experience my first meeting. At this stage, I had little idea of what the meeting would be like. My only experience had been the rather formal services in the prison chapel. This was anything but formal. A guitar provided the music and the singing was loud and enthusiastic. They loved to sing the great old hymns of the church. The prayers were sincere, unpolished and from the heart; all very strange to a newcomer like myself. Darril Dowden, the resident pastor, led the meeting. In such a situation, my instinct would be to sit on the back row, keep my head down and observe. However, one of the lads took me to the front row to sit with him. In this rather exposed position, I felt obliged at least to stand up with the others and join in the singing. After all, I had a reasonable voice. The hymns weren't exactly my sort of music, but I followed the words projected on the screen before us and did my best.

After a spell of singing, they began to worship God and suddenly the whole atmosphere changed dramatically. I immediately knew this was something different and it grabbed my full attention. Around me the boys were praying earnestly with their hands raised, tears running down the faces of many. This really got to me. I kept looking round and thinking, *"What's going on? This is weird."* As with the singing, out of respect, I thought that I ought to close my eyes, so I did. As I stood there I began to think about Jesus and the stuff I had read in prison. I wondered what He looked like. I thought, *"I don't know what He looks like."* At this point, the only image of Jesus I had ever seen came powerfully to my mind. Opposite Llanelli Police Station there is a Catholic church. Outside the church there is a cross with a representation of

Jesus on it. From my frequent visits to the station I had a memory of this crucifix, which I could clearly see when leaving. Later, some pastors and leaders I met disliked me telling this part of my story because they don't have crucifixes and the like in their churches. All I know is that in this particular experience, God used that image to speak to me.

As I stood there with eyes tight shut, that image of Jesus on the cross came alive in a vision and it was as if I was actually there, at the cross, as Jesus was crucified. I saw His wounds, the blood, the darkened sky. It was all very real. Then as I looked at the crown of thorns, Jesus lifted His head and looked at me. I saw His eyes and they seemed to pierce my soul. He simply spoke one sentence: "Richard, I did this for you." I just broke. The tears began to flow. My eyes were still closed so I didn't know what was going on around me. I just said, "Lord, I give my life to You." This was my response. I didn't pray any special prayer or put up my hand in a meeting to respond to a preacher. I saw a vision of Jesus and I knew it was Him. It was a response that came from the depths of my being with absolute and total sincerity. A strong conviction about sin came over me from the Holy Spirit and I knew without being told by anyone that it was my sin, things that I had done, that had nailed Him to the cross. I felt so guilty. I know now that there is nothing we can do to repay Jesus for the sacrifice He made. However, at this moment, I felt that I wanted to do something. The least I could do was to surrender my life to Him. This only lasted a few moments before I felt my sin being taken from me. It felt like God was taking a cloth and wiping away my sin and then rinsing the cloth before wiping again and again until I was clean inside.

A few more moments passed, followed by a strange feeling that the top of my head was opened and warm oil poured in.

I felt the oil going down through my body, reaching every part. I was filled up and up until the level reached my mouth and I wanted to say, "Thank You Jesus, thank You God," but it came out in another language. Up to this point I had never heard of speaking in tongues and certainly never heard anyone speaking in this way. I had heard the term "Pentecostal" but had no idea to what it referred. It could have been a brand of detergent for all I knew. Now I was really freaked out. What on earth was going on? But the more I spoke in this language, the better I felt. It was like taking drugs. I know it sounds weird, but the same buzz I got from drugs, I had from speaking in this language. Without being conscious of raising my hands, they were up. It was as if someone had lifted them. I fell to my knees and then flopped over until I was curled up on the floor in a foetal position crying like a baby.

Eventually I got up staggering a bit as if I was drunk. I grabbed hold of the pastor by his lapels and said, "What happened to me?" His answer was, "Richard, you have been born again and filled with the Holy Spirit." He picked up his Bible and while everyone else was still praising, showed me some verses from the book of Acts chapter 2 about the coming of the Holy Spirit. "This is what has happened to you." I looked around at everyone, not knowing what to do next – so I went outside for a cigarette! I may have had an incredible spiritual experience, but I wanted to ponder what had happened to me. The best way to do that was to go out and smoke. I took out a cigarette and lit it. As I inhaled the smoke, I had the strange sensation that it was coming out of the back of my head! It wasn't, but that's how it felt. The nicotine had no effect on me. I thought that there must be something wrong with the cigarette, so I stubbed it out and lit another. The same thing happened. This time I stubbed it out, took out the whole packet, threw it on the floor and ground it up with my heel. Later I spoke to Dinah about it and told her I wanted to give up smoking. She simply replied, "If you don't want to smoke, don't smoke." I have never smoked a cigarette since, nor had any desire to.

I returned to the meeting and Darril was preaching about the cross. The things he said all confirmed my experience. Later, over a coffee, I tried to explain to everyone the details of my experience. Everyone was rejoicing, some were crying, I was on a real high. I went to the office and gave Dinah a big hug and thanked her for letting me come to live in this community. That night I couldn't sleep, I just wanted to question my room-mate about his experience. They then moved me to a different room and I shared with Simon Mole who was more advanced in his Christian faith and a member of staff. He was better equipped to answer the many questions that I had. His background was similar to mine and this helped me to identify with him. He told me about miracles he had seen. I believed him; after what had happened to me, anything was possible.

My first miracle came sooner than I expected. Technically, I was still a drug addict. I needed a regular fix or I was a mess. But one day went by, then another, and I wasn't experiencing any withdrawal or craving. I was amazed; I no longer wanted drugs. It came as a beautiful breaking dawn, the realisation that I no longer needed speed, heroin, cannabis or anything else. Both mentally and physically, I was absolutely free. Had I needed any further proof that God was real and was doing something amazing in me, this was it. Very importantly, my mind was also free from the daily treadmill of scheming to get money and drugs. With the removal of the thing that had dominated my mind for so long, there remained a sort of void, spare capacity to think of other things. My addictive personality adopted a new passion; I became totally hooked on the Bible. I simply replaced one addiction with another – a more constructive one.

With the same vigour that I had pursued drugs, I now read and studied the Bible. I read for hours at a time. Sometimes I had to be called for meals because I was in my room reading, oblivious to time. Someone would knock and say, "C'mon Rich, it's dinner time." "I'll be there in five minutes, I just want to finish this," was a typical response. I would put my Bible down, go and eat my meal, then return immediately to where I had left off. Four times a day I listened avidly to the Bible being preached. I wasn't used to reading much and could not be described as a speed-reader. Nevertheless, I read the Bible cover to cover three times in my first year as a Christian; it was very intense. Sometimes I hardly talked to anyone. I just wanted to talk to God and read. I was still only eighteen years old.

Epilogue

Richard returned to the Crown Court for sentence and was given two years' probation allowing him to stay at Victory Outreach. Whilst still at Victory Outreach, Richard began to travel sharing his testimony and was soon invited to preach at local churches. Later he began receiving invitations to preach at larger churches and shared the Gospel passionately seeing many people respond and come to Christ. After leaving Victory Outreach he went on to study for a degree in theology at the Birmingham Bible Institute and began to pastor a small church in Tipton in the West Midlands. Today Richard is the Associate Pastor of Renewal Christian Centre in Solihull, one of the fastest growing Charismatic churches in the UK. He is married to Jill and they have three sons. Richard co-presented the BBC prime time television series, *To Catch a Thief* and has since appeared as a guest on numerous radio and TV programmes.

A final word...

Thank you for reading my story. Like you, the history of my life continues to be written. I realise one thing, that no matter who you are or what you have done, God loves you more than words can express. Reading about my life may have challenged you to think about your own relationship with God. I want you to know that God is only one prayer away. He can transform your life and give you a future that you could never have imagined. Give God a chance to prove Himself in your life today. If you want to know more about God and how you can get to know Him, please contact me:

Rev. Richard Taylor
Renewal Christian Centre
Lode Lane
Solihull
West Midlands
B91 2JR

Tel: 0121 711 7300
Email: church@renewalcc.com

Have you ever felt like faith was working for others but not for you?

This book explores the biblical principles of faith. Its fresh approach with practical application will help you to put your faith to work in everyday life and aspire to greater things in God. There is no formula to faith, but faith does have a process: *hear it, see it, say it, and seize it* – these four areas are fundamental for our faith to work effectively.

"Richard's book addresses the importance of good faith practice and illustrates in simple, practical ways the journey from belief to faith. This book will be a great help to all who read it."
Paul Weaver, General Superintendent, Assemblies of God, UK

"Faith is a much preached subject with many failsafe formulas. This book however, walks the reader though the dynamics of living in biblical faith daily. It will show you how to live in faith and be free to become part of your dreams."
David Carr, Regional Overseer Free Methodist Church, Senior Pastor, Renewal Christian Centre, Solihull, UK

"This book, written by a 'faith practitioner', will help believers to be strengthened in their faith, please the Lord, and be effective in their Christian witness. I heartily recommend it."
Wynne Lewis, International Ministry
Former General Superintendent for Elim Churches UK, and Senior Pastor, Kensington Temple, London, UK

New Wine Press
ISBN 1 903725 43 7
£6.99

We hope you enjoyed reading this New Wine book.
For details of other New Wine books and
a range of 2,000 titles from other
Word and Spirit publishers visit our website:
www.newwineministries.co.uk